GESTALT
RECONSIDERED

GESTALT INSTITUTE OF CLEVELAND PRESS

THE NEUROTIC BEHAVIOR OF ORGANIZATIONS
Uri Merry and George Brown

BODY PROCESS: A GESTALT APPROACH TO WORKING
WITH THE BODY IN PSYCHOTHERAPY
James I. Kepner

ORGANIZATIONAL CONSULTING: A GESTALT APPROACH
Edwin C. Nevis

GESTALT RECONSIDERED: A NEW APPROACH
TO CONTACT AND RESISTANCE
Gordon Wheeler

GESTALT RECONSIDERED

A New Approach to Contact and Resistance

GORDON WHEELER, Ph.D.

press

The Gestalt Institute of Cleveland Press

PUBLISHED BY

Gardner Press, Inc.

New York   Sydney   London

Gestalt Institute of Cleveland Press
Published and Distributed by Gardner Press

GARDNER PRESS, INC.
19 UNION SQUARE WEST
NEW YORK, NEW YORK 10003

All foreign orders except Canada and South America to:

Afterhurst Limited
Chancery House
319 City Road
London, N1, United Kingdom

Library of Congress Cataloging-in-Publication Data

Wheeler, Gordon, 1949-
    Gestalt reconsidered : a new approach to contact and resistance / by
Gordon Wheeler.
        p.   cm.
    Includes bibliographical references.
    ISBN 0-89876-159-X : $24.95
    1. Gestalt therapy.   2. Resistance (Psychoanalysis)   3. Gestalt
therapy—Case studies.   I. Title.
RC489.G4W44   1990
616.89'143—dc20   90-32243
                                                                CIP

Design by Publishers Creative Services

FOR BEVERLY —
FIGURE AND GROUND

CONTENTS

>> Contents <<

AN INTRODUCTION, AS Erik Erikson has observed, is an author's chance to put his or her afterthoughts first. In Gestalt terms, this makes for a contact boundary of a particular kind, charged and organized in particular ways, between author and reader, just before plunging into the material ahead. On the one hand there is the author, just back, so to speak, from the territory that still lies more or less hidden from the reader, caught at a moment of withdrawal or reflection after that journey, and oriented by the feelings and concerns that belong to that phase of the contact cycle: satisfaction perhaps, and a gathering excitement about sharing the journey with another person, but also quite possibly sadness and loss, apprehension about others' reception of this presentation of self, proprietorship and protection, even an anticipatory defensiveness—all those sensations and feelings, in short, that may go along with what Paul Goodman taught us to call the *resistance of egotism*, that fear of loss or damage to the self, a last-ditch attempt to hold back from, or control at least, the crucial moment of letting go, which is the encounter itself.

And on the other hand, there is the reader, at an entirely different point in the rhythm of engagement or contact, and with quite another agenda of felt desires, needs, apprehensions, which will organize the ground of the figure of contact of the moment and in turn shape the approach to the larger contact ahead. Attention or distraction, excitement or relative indifference, openness or caution, suspicion, trust, compliance with authority, the defensiveness or giving of the self to the encounter mentioned above on the author's side—all of these, in all their possible blends and shadings, enter into the dynamic organization of the reader's *contact boundary*, which, as Goodman says, is not a point or place but rather a process, the "organ of a particular relationship," which is contact itself (F. Perls, Hefferline, & Goodman, 1951, p. 269). To paraphrase Kurt Lewin (and thereby anticipate the argument of Chapter I), the *felt purpose or need* will organize the encounter on both sides—within the given conditions, and with the support or constraint of each person's own particular capacity for a flexible *range* of attitudes, or styles of approach, appropriate to those felt goals and conditions (which is in turn the particular subject matter of psychotherapy).

In other words, a few brief strokes and already we have suggested the outlines, at least, of a contact moment which is complexly organized and richly political (in the sense of having to do with relationship or influence), and very far indeed from the Perls/Goodman Platonic ideal of a "clear bright figure freely energized from an *empty* background" (emphasis added; F. Perls et al., 1951, p. 299). And the main event hasn't even begun yet!

Small wonder then, under the given contact conditions, which is to say the background goals and structures on both sides, if authors commonly try to use introductions to prestructure, or influence if possible, the outcome of the fuller contact ahead, which is the encounter with the main text itself. Generally this attempt takes the form of a sort of guided tour, or preview, of the landscape yet to come, pointing out various attractive features, minimizing or sidestepping the pitfalls, and especially indicating where the reader should come out on the other side, and what the right route is for getting there. Fair enough, but it should be clear by now that this is no ordinary roadmap, such as might be given to the innocent traveler by some well-meaning yet dispassionate guide—if such a thing existed!—but rather is itself a highly partisan document, an invitation to "map" the contact process itself in certain ways and not others, according to certain pre-agreed features of the ground. And here again, in only a few brief paragraphs we have arrived at one of the fundamental cornerstones of the Goodman/Perls philosophical critique of "establishment" psychotherapy of the time: namely, the *radical, positive reevaluation of passionate desire*, as the essential pathway to truth and right action—in sharp contradiction to both the classical Freudian and, for that matter, the Eastern mystical views, of enlightenment through objectivity, sublimation, or detachment. Likewise, on the reader's side (and in anticipation of much of the argument below), let us recognize and honor her or his resistance as the very sign of passionate or mobilized engagement, in the process of contact itself—and not as a block or subversion of that process.

So far so good, but there is at least one further risk to this sort of partisan preview, which is that in the course of mapping out the terrain ahead, and trying to make the various stages of the journey seem to follow seamlessly and inevitably one after the other, it may well be that the whole argument of the book takes on a more tightly logical character, a more linear appearance, than it had in its original development, which may have been more organic, more back-and-forth, from central idea to component parts—in a word, more "Gestalt." In the process, it may happen that the most basic thesis of a book, the central energizing idea that infuses and organizes the parts, is nowhere stated clearly (as the reassessment of *desire*, which underlies Volume II of *Gestalt Therapy*, is not directly discussed in that book). Let us state, then, that central organizing idea before proceeding with the roadmap of the chapters to come: namely, that the model of contact handed down to us by Goodman and Perls, and elaborated by many subsequent authors, is *figure-bound*, in a theoretical sense; that the analysis of this contact process (or awareness, or experience) is incomplete without direct consideration of *organized features or structures of ground*, enduring in some cases across situations and over time, that infuse and constrain the figures of contact themselves; that psychotherapy (or any change induction process) is always a matter of reorganization of these structures of ground over time, and not merely of contact figures of the moment; that the Gestalt model, theoretically at least, has been hampered by this overemphasis on figure from addressing a full range of clinical and systemic problems; that the Goodman/Perls model contains certain distortions or internal contradictions which have worked against development of this full potential; and finally, that the revision of these contradictory propositions permits the emergence of a model with certain new capacities—namely, the reevaluation of "resistances," and the possibility of addressing "clinical" and "organizational" problems for the first time in the same theoretical terms. All of these are formulations of the same basic idea, which is the *focusing of direct attention, in Gestalt analysis, on the ques-*

tion of structures of ground. To focus that attention is the purpose of this book.

To set the stage for this discussion, and in the process indicate certain theoretical roads not taken, we will first of all go back to the early part of this century, in Chapter I, to consider some of the fascinating, revolutionary work of the first generation of academic Gestalt psychologists, principally Wertheimer, Koffka, Kohler, and their followers—work so radically influential that it is impossible to conceive of any psychology at all today, even the most thoroughgoing "behaviorism," which is not fundamentally Gestalt in nature. From there we will take up the outgrowth of this work in the concerns of the second generation of the "Gestalt School," particularly Lewin and Goldstein—not because their far-reaching elaborations of the original perceptual model into the domains of personality and behavior directly influenced the Good-man/Perls model, but because, curiously enough, they did not— for reasons considered more directly in Chapters II and III. In all of this we will be arguing in conscious opposition to the positions of Henle (1978), Arnheim (1949), and (sometimes) Perls himself (see for example 1969b), all of whom have maintained that connections between Gestalt psychology per se and the Gestalt therapy model are either not centrally important or else wholly nonexistent. On the contrary, in Chapter I (and the succeeding chapters) we will try to show that the connections are direct and essential, if not always fully developed. Perls himself first sensed this link, even if he failed to articulate it clearly, in his early collaborative work with his wife Laura, *Ego, Hunger and Aggression* (F. Perls, 1947).

It is to this early work of Perls that we will turn our attention directly in Chapter II. From the point of view of the later Gestalt model, the book, to use the author's own word, is "sketchy" at best: the Gestalt ideas promised at the outset are nowhere developed through most of the text, and when at last they are touched upon, briefly, at the end, the connection with a Gestalt perspective is not made clear. For these reasons, a disclaimer at this point may be in order, at the risk of belaboring what is beyond contention: namely, that there would be no Gestalt therapy model without Fritz Perls. It was Perls, as just mentioned above, who first "sniffed" the implications of a Gestalt view of awareness, for a new approach to personality and psychotherapy (true, those implications were pregnantly present, as argued in Chapter I, in the earlier work of Lewin and Goldstein, but Perls may have been unaware of Lewin, and by his own account [1969b], he did not understand Goldstein's work until many years later). It was Perls, together with Laura Perls, who drew together the study group that gave birth to the Gestalt therapy model itself, in New York in the years immediately after World War II. And it was Perls, by all accounts, who gave Paul Goodman an original monograph, which was the jumping-off point, at least, of Goodman's fuller theoretical presentation in 1951. Readers of this chapter who knew Perls have generally commented that something essential of the man himself —his presence, his commitment to liveliness and authenticity, his own particular kind of integrity or wholeness—does not come through in this more purely theoretical critique. Perls stood, in the words of Ed Nevis, for a "whole new way of being in the world," of listening for and honoring what was true within, before the closure of a premature resignation about what was possible, or practical, or readily acceptable socially. Perhaps it is inevitable for those of us in a later generation who did not have the chance to be moved by Perls personally that something of the inspirational force of the contact should be lost on the page. Suffice it to say here that when we speak of Perls in the chapters below, we mean Perls the writer, and more specifically the actual written work he left behind—none too extensive, in comparison with his actual influence on contemporary psychotherapy—and not the man himself.

Turning to Chapter III, the work of Goodman (in indeterminate collaboration with Perls and others), we will have arrived at last at a full-scale model of Gestalt therapy itself—or at any rate a full theoretical rationale for such a model, and a suggestion of what that model might look like in application over time (to a degree not always appreciated in the Gestalt literature, it was left to other writers and teachers, notably Laura Perls, Isdore From, Erv and Miriam Polster, Joseph Zinker, and many others to do the demanding theoretical and practical work of developing this rationale into a clinical and educational methodology, with of course many extensions and refinements along the way). But who is the author of this original presentation? Goodman claimed authorship, from a basis of a preliminary monograph of Perls's (Wysong, 1985), and publicly, at least, this claim seems never to have been disputed (though Joel Latner, for one, does assert that Perls's original manuscript was somewhat more elaborated and closer to the final version than Goodman would seem to allow; Latner, personal communication to E. Nevis, 1988). However this may be, a comparison of published texts does seem sufficient to establish that the authorial *voice* of *Gestalt Therapy*, Vol. II is Goodman's—regardless of how collaborative the thinking that lay behind the voice itself. The figure, we may say, is Goodman, though the ground certainly included Perls, Laura Perls, and others as well. Moreover, there are certain clear discrepancies of emphasis, at least, between the exposition here and other work published under Perls's name, both before and after—which again reveal the organizing hand of Goodman in this volume. And finally, there are both discrepancies and some outright contradictions between Volume I and Volume II of the book (some of which are discussed in detail in Chapter III)— all of which again supports Goodman's contention that he "wrote" the second volume, in a different sense from that in which he contributed to the first. Therefore, in this chapter and throughout the book, when we use the formulation "Goodman said," or variations on it, we will understand that to mean *at least* that Goodman himself subscribed to the particular proposition or argument in question, since it appears in his voice—without prejudice to the question of whether the coauthors did or did not share that particular view, or what share they had, exactly, in generating it.

Chapter IV will take up directly some of the "extensions and refinements" mentioned above—in particular those of what we will be calling the Cleveland School, itself constituting a diverse body of work which is nevertheless united by certain recurrent themes and concerns. A theory, as suggested above, is not necessarily a method, though it may contain one, and either may imply the other. It is one thing to say, as Goodman does, that the new therapy will attend to the "internal structure of the actual experience" (Perls et al., 1951, p. 273), and quite another to lay out in practical and theoretical detail exactly *how* that is to be done, by what method, and with what sequence of interventions on the therapist's part. Again, it was the writers of the Cleveland School— including especially the Nevises, the Polsters, Zinker, and others— who undertook the creative labor of articulating this methodology (in the literal sense of identifying joints, or points of boundary and connection). As Goodman is to Perls, in the sense of taking a brilliant initial insight and working it into a full and coherent theoretical statement, so the Cleveland writers, over the past four decades, have been, in a sense, to Goodman. Thus the classic work of the Polsters, outlining what is *meant*, in the Gestalt sense, by contact and the resistances; of Zinker, with his deeply insightful and carefully dramatic elaboration of the Gestalt experiment; or the Nevises, with their extensions of the model into applications to multiperson systems.

In many of these written works and much of their teaching, writers of the Cleveland group and others (like their teachers Laura Perls and Isadore From) have sometimes raised many of the same concerns and misgivings about certain parts of the received theory that constitute the central subject of this book. As befits a methodology-building stage of theory development, their answer, in some cases, was to address the problems in terms of method itself. Thus issues such as group and social ground, intimate commitment, the creative uses of "resistances," problems of "character" and "personality," the use of personal history in psychotherapy, are frequent themes in this body of writing and teaching. What we would add now, at a later stage in a wider theory-building cycle, is the direct focus of attention on those areas of the original model that make it hard to address these concerns in a consistent and fully practical way, and those neglected extensions of academic Gestalt psychology into these realms that would support those concerns.

In Chapter V, we turn to the integration of all that has gone before: the use of the Lewinian and Goldsteinian models to develop the concept of structured ground; the consequences of this organizational approach for the awareness theory of change and change induction; the resultant shift of emphasis in the definition of contact itself; the revised understanding of the "resistances" that flows from this shift (revised theoretically; in practice this revision, we will argue, has been around for a long time); and the integrated model itself, which, we will be claiming, can address the full range of human and clinical problems outlined above in a more consistent, more flexible, more fully "Gestalt" way. To repeat, far from being taken up in an "anti-Perls" or "anti-Goodman" spirit, these arguments are intended to return us to the basic premises of their model, by way of addressing certain incomplete or neglected features of that model, which are more salient, more figural, in our time than in theirs. And finally, along the way, as a methodological dividend, so to speak, of the insistence on starting with ground, not figure, we will come out with a model, by these arguments, which can at last address intrapsychic and interpersonal or systemic problems *in the same theoretical language*— something that has been eluding clinicians, among others, since the time of Freud.

And with this, our (partisan) preview of the territory ahead is virtually complete. (Whether the arguments presented in these five chapters are complete or not lies with the reader to judge.) In general, with the exception of certain illustrative material from early Gestalt research in Chapter I, case examples and narrative vignettes have been kept out of the text up to this point, in hopes of achieving a narrative rhythm and clarity of a different, more theoretical kind. On the one hand, each chapter is intended to be able to stand alone, and the reader who is more interested in one topic than another should be able to read any single chapter— or for that matter all the chapters in any order—and still get the gist, at least, of the overall argument, which is recapitulated in each new stage of its presentation. On the other hand, each successive chapter attempts to take up this theoretical narrative and advance it in the direction outlined above (and note the tone of partisan linearity, creeping back into the tour guide at this point). With the final two chapters, in hopes of redressing this theory/practice imbalance at least to some extent, two groups of cases are presented, one group in the "clinical" area and the other in the social or organizational domain (keeping in mind that with the revisions developed through the previous chapters, it should be possible to address these different "levels" of a problem in the same terms). To repeat a point already mentioned here, and frequently reiterated in the chapters ahead, we are not claiming to be the first to do this under the Gestalt model. Rather, the position here is that the best and most creative Gestalt practice is *already doing* many or most of the things advocated under this theoretical revision. But, by the contention here, "best practice" in the Gestalt model is not everywhere supported by theory, but is forced to make certain habitual leaps, unexplained reversals, or fuzzy connections. This is all very well if you know what you are doing, but it is very hard to teach! Thus, in a real sense, it is Gestalt *teaching* that this book most hopes to influence, with the aim of supporting and passing on that creative practice, out of a better-organized theoretical ground.

And an (almost) final word, again about Goodman and Perls. It is commonplace for revisionists to claim that they are returning to the basics, which have somehow become lost or distorted over time—or even that they are uniquely placed to explain what the masters *really* meant, better than those masters could themselves. It is also commonplace, these days, to take note of the fact that much of Perls's work, particularly in later years, was a theatrical display of only one corner, so to speak, of the Gestalt model he had been so instrumental in developing, and that if not actually a caricature of that model, some of this work quickly lent itself to caricature in the hands of other, less disciplined showmen (and showwomen). Like a Hokusai simplifying his brushwork with age, Perls used shortcuts and rapid strokes that quickly became lifeless clichés in the hands of some of his imitators, who saw them not as grounded leaps to the heart of the impasse, but short circuits around a necessary lifetime of clinical and cultural experience. Thus the common practice, nowadays, of taking a few ritual easy shots at Perls by way of distancing one's own position from a certain kind of "Gestalt" practice that has fallen into well-deserved ill-repute. *That is not the intent of this presentation,* nor is that the view of Perls himself espoused here, whatever the differences of theoretical emphasis developed in these chapters, and however inadequate the presentation, particularly in Chapter II, of Perls-the-clinician and Perls-the-man. Perls, in spite of the contradictions in his life and his theoretical perspective, stood always and clearly, figure-and-ground, for authenticity, liveliness, and adventure (in the true sense, of risking the self in the encounter). This is not to say he would have endorsed all the arguments of this book. But he certainly would, if he had lived, say, another ten or fifteen years, have turned his famous impatience and his withering eye on the common clinical problems of these days, which we have been identifying as distortions not just of figure, but of structured ground: anomie, consumerism, me-firstism, lack of commitment, personal and political, and those related problems of the *unpassionate heart* that present so frequently in the clinical (and non-clinical) population of our times. One imagines, with relish, some hapless latter-day hot-seat victim, under the lash of the famous Persian scorn: "Get out of here! I can't work with you. You're not committed to *anything.*"

Likewise, and more so, for Paul Goodman. Today, after the near-total eclipse of Goodman's literary and political/philosophical work, it is only a matter of time until he is again recognized for what he was and is: namely, one of the centrally influential, critically intellectual voices of the "American Mid-Century," and one of its exemplary stylists. To echo the text ahead, it has been an immeasurable loss for Gestalt therapy, and a tragic one for our times, that Goodman did not live to bring his obsidian eloquence and his vast intellectual resources to bear on the different problems (or different manifestations of the same problem) of the individual-in-society in our times. It is easy to forget today that Goodman, while prophetically critical, was by no means a voice crying in the wilderness in his own day. On the contrary, he was enormously, directly influential in the whole range of liberation movements of the fifties and sixties—including the movement to liberate psychotherapy from the stale confines of the Freudian training institutes (today so much less stale, partly because of the competitive influence of the Gestalt model), and not least in his influence on the shaping of the mind of a whole generation that would trust its own visceral repugnance to an obscene war, in opposition to all the authoritarian force of the day. Goodman, if he were alive at this writing, would be only as old as the current President of the United States. Even to voice the comparison is to cry out at what this society is capable of doing to the very best of its men and women.

And a penultimate word, on usage. People come, with only the very rarest exceptions, in definite genders, one or the other. The English language, however, provides only the feminine gender with a set of pronouns all its own, while the masculine set does triple duty, for the male, the collective, and sometimes the impersonal cases. Exactly to whose disadvantage this works most is unclear, as with so many things in gender politics. Meanwhile, the cumbersomeness of always repeating the locutions "he or she," "her and his," and so forth, is already apparent in this introduction. At the same time, the use of *they* and *their* to refer to the singular impersonal *everyone* is confusing and unacceptable. Therefore, with apologies to all sides, and in hopes of better times in the language and in the culture, in this text the unsatisfactory traditional practice will be followed, of using *he*, *his*, and *him* to cover both the masculine and the general case.

Finally, this book, like any book, is a conversation, or one side of a conversation, which is continued in the reader's mind, and then completed, if the author is lucky, in some ongoing expression of response. But this conversation itself is the outgrowth of many, many past conversations, which have entered and organized the ground for this figure. Thanks go to the following past conversational partners—teachers, students, colleagues, and friends—for their creative agreement and disagreement, challenge and support, all of which have infused and informed the present figure of contact: Anne Alonso, Norm Berkowitz, Rennie Fantz, Isadore From, Murray Horwitz, Michel Katzeff, Frank Kelly, Carolyn Lukensmeyer, Bert Moore, Ed Nevis, Sonia Nevis, Bernie O'Brien, Patricia Papernow, Erv Polster, Jean-Marie Robine, the late Bill Warner, Joseph Zinker, and Walter Grossman, mentor and living model of the Goodman ideal of a passionate intellectual, and a complete man; and most of all to my professional, conversational, and life partner, Beverly Reifman.

I

The Background in Gestalt Psychology

GESTALT AND THE ASSOCIATIONIST MODEL

GESTALT PSYCHOLOGY was conceived, according to the legend, on a train somewhere between Hannover and Frankfurt-am-Main, in 1910 (the exact date and hour could no doubt be reconstructed), when the psychologist Max Wertheimer fell to musing on the optical behavior of the lines and poles of the telegraph system running alongside the tracks (M. M. Wertheimer, 1964). Accordingly as the train sped up or slowed down, the poles would appear to be first of all what they were (i.e., separate poles, in series), then a single pole, looming forward and back in un-dulating motion, and then again a single pole frozen at a particular spot outside the window, while the wires themselves might take on the appearance of a stationary wire, only waving up and down. Still according to legend, Wertheimer left the train at Frankfurt, entered a toy shop, and purchased a child's stroboscopic device, the better to study these familiar yet peculiar effects, which did not seem at all well accounted for under the prevailing reflex or Associationist school of psychological thought. The result, two years later, was a paper, "Experimentelle Studien ueber das Sehen von Bewegungen" ("Experimental Studies in the Perception of Motion," M. Wertheimer, 1912), in which he propounded the concept of a "Phi" factor, or integrative principle, by which the organism translated individual, serial sense impressions into a unified perception of continuous motion; thus the Gestalt school was born.

In reality, of course, development was much more gradual in both directions, forward and back, as is always the case with any theoretical breakthrough—more atomistic, or "associationist," in contrast to this highly "gestalt" myth of a single moment of Newtonian insight. The problem of atomized versus continuous perception goes back at least to Zeno, in the fifth century B.C., with his famous paradox of the tortoise and the hare (since the tortoise always moves ahead, by however small an amount, during the same time it takes the hare to catch up to where the tortoise was before, therefore, logically speaking, it would seem that the hare can never actually *pass* the tortoise). The difficulty here is the seeming incommensurability of fragmented and continuous processes, no matter how small the fragments you break the perceptual phenomenon in question down to (as the Associationist model hoped to do). In mathematics, this problem was not resolved theoretically for another couple of thousand years, until Newton's and Leibniz's invention of the calculus—the mathematics of continuous functions. In psychology, the use of the term "gestalt" itself, in addressing these and other problems of the Associationist approach, goes back at least to Ehrenfels, in 1890 (it was also Ehrenfels who introduced the terms "figure" and "ground" to perceptual psychology; Koffka, 1935). Mach himself, generally regarded as the founder of modern psychology, was concerned not just with "pure associationist" or stimulus-reflex patterns in research, but also with the broader question of how it is that things appear to us as they do (Petermann, 1932, p. 3). Likewise, Schumann (1900), Mueller (1923), Krueger (1913, 1915), and especially Martius (1912) had all addressed themselves to the quality of "wholeness" in perception, variously criticizing the "atomistic" theory that perception is merely the sum of a set of individual stimuli, each of which presumably activates a particular brain cell or cells—using such unifying terms as "production," "coherence theory," "complex quality," and even "gestalt quality." Exner, writing in 1894 (the same year in which Freud first mentions the "defenses," another "whole configuration" of functioning with which we will be much concerned in the chapters to follow), offers this: "The whole impression produced by a picture which flashes across the retina is made up of the excitations of innumerable and functionally dissimilar fibres. That we, in spite of this, form a unitary impression, in which the separate sensations remain unnoted, is due to what I would call the Principle of Central Confluence" (p. 201, author's translation). Exner's Central Confluence is certainly very close to Wertheimer's Phi factor, some twenty years later.

Under the terms of the "Wundt school," or pure Associationist theory, dominant at the turn of the century, perception should proceed as follows: a particular, discrete stimulus in the environment—say, a particular frequency and intensity of light, given off by a certain object and measurable by physical devices—strikes the retina at a certain angle and energy level. This activates a further neurological sequence, step by step, ending in the stimulation of particular brain cells or patterns of cells, which then either "produce" or somehow themselves "are" the mental image (the model is a little fuzzy on this crucial point; see discussion in Koffka, 1935; also Kohler, 1947). Thus, the theory is "reductionist" in both directions: i.e., the mental event can be exactly reduced to the physical event "outside," and vice versa. In theory at least, there should be an exact, one-to-one correspondence between external object and internal image (or at least between internal image and what the Associationists called the "proximate stimulus," that is in this case the actual amount and quality of light striking the retinal surface—since obviously the "thing itself" may vary, as a stimulus, under differing conditions of lighting, distance, air quality, motion, and so forth).

To the question, how can a quite finite number of retinal cells account for such an astonishingly large array of mental imagery, the Associationist answer is, through recombination and permutation of independent elements—i.e., cells. The image here is like, let us say, the telephone network of a large city, where the recombination of as few as ten simple stimulus elements, in uniformly varying little chains of seven elements each, easily gives you all the phone connections in, say, New York City, with its millions upon millions of various possibilities, not to mention the potential for functional elaboration, conference calls, call forwarding, call waiting, even operator assistance, and other possibilities for relinking the chains themselves. Add three more elements and you get all of North America; another five or so will give you the world. Thus it is possible, so the Associationist argument would go, to build up constructs and complex memories, even abstract ideas and problem-solving patterns, out of a limited number of simple, unitary, discrete "building blocks" in complex recombination, without the introduction of vague and tautological "ghosts in the machine" to explain how the elements get organized.

Given these assumptions, it is natural that much of the lab research under this paradigm tended to focus on the phrenological: that is, where exactly in the brain could the pathways and particular cells be found in which particular sense impressions were "stored," and how were these cells linked to others, in a stimulus-response way (for a discussion of this type of metaphor as a research guide in Associationism, see Goldstein, 1939, 1940; also Koffka, 1935, especially chap. III). A great deal of this work, as Goldstein pointed out (1939), was actually not conducted *in vivo* at all, but had to do rather with reflex patterns of nervous tissue *in vitro*, or with the nerve reactions of decorticated—i.e., brain-dead—lab animals, which do indeed demonstrate the kind of pure "stimulus-bound" reaction patterns of the Associationist model, much as Goldstein was later to find in frontal-lobe cases of certain brain-damaged war veterans. Thus, as always in science, the working paradigm tends to control the research approach—a phenomenon which is itself best explained by Gestalt psychology. The underlying assumptions of the model, often unexamined, will critically determine the conditions and procedures of research, and the kinds of questions asked—and thus the findings, which may then reinforce the model. That Gestalt research itself was not to be immune to this kind of unexamined assumption will become evident in the discussion below.

Now the trouble with this kind of "networking" or "wiring" model as an explanatory metaphor in Associationism is that for the analogy to be useful, the brain would have to be thought of as containing not just the telephone network alone, with its miles

15

and miles of cable and all the various switching functions, but in a sense all the *subscribers* to the system as well; not just the wiring but the messages on the wires, the conversations, images, processes, interactions, all of which are also somehow "within" the brain, and seemingly in an organized and manipulable fashion. At this point the Associationist metaphor begins to break down, and one is tempted to ask how such a simplistic and seemingly naive view of mental life could ever have been expected to generate useful and complete explanations for complex, abstract mental functions, which seem to take place at quite a far remove, on some qualitatively different level, from any "proximate stimulus" at all.

In all fairness, and despite some of the excessive claims of latter-day behaviorists, the original model itself probably never had any such pretensions. Associationism, originally at any rate, was first of all an attempt to clear away some of the tautological or "mentalistic" deadwood which psychology had carried over with it from philosophy, of which it was still a branch, as recently as a century ago (chiefly Aristotelian constructs ascribing movements to motility, purpose to purposefulness, will to intentionality, and the like). Still, in their attempt to move away from the endless generation of explanations-in-a-circle, the Associationsts (as the above citations indicate) were themselves very much aware of some of the limitations of their own theory (see also Mandler & Mandler, 1964), and were constantly producing second- and third-order constructs of their own, such as learning, experience, interpretation, selective attention, and emotionality, to explain the apparent transformations of sense data after it "entered" the nervous system (Koffka, 1935). If the model continued to hold sway as long as it did (see Petermann, 1932, for perhaps the latest systematic defense), this was probably for two basic reasons. First is the plain fact that sensation and perception and thinking must obviously all be in *some* way connected with the world of "real" external stimuli, or else it is hard to see how the organism could ever interact successfully with the environment, even imperfectly. And second, the scientific/philosophical links between the Associationist model and Newtonian physics, which offered such a simple and satisfying reduction of the complex world of phenomena into a few underlying elementary forces and particles, along the same lines as the Associationist paradigm. In the Newtonian model, in theory at least, if ever you could once get through cataloguing the exact position and velocity of every last discrete particle of elementary "stuff" in the universe,—why, then you would automatically know, potentially at least, not only everything that was "happening" anywhere in the universe at a given time, but also everything that ever had happened, and everything that ever would. Practically speaking, of course, you might never get all the coordinates plotted out. Still, there would be no *theoretical* obstacle to total knowledge, only one of time and resources. In short, the secrets of the universe had been unlocked, and man was rapidly stepping toward a position of omniscience with regard to the physical world. If the mental world could only be conquered as well, then the position would be godlike indeed.

The seductive power of this model of conquest and control is obvious; even today we can still feel it as an intoxicating if lost dream. Lost, because ironically the very physics which the early psychologists (and some not so early) took as their touchstone and their guide was even then on the verge of being swept away—first by general relativity theory, after the turn of the century, and then more devastatingly, in the twenties, by Heisenberg's Uncertainty Principle, which claimed to demonstrate that such absolute knowledge was unattainable, by its very nature.

Nonetheless, and whatever the inadequacies of the Associationist model against which the Gestalt school was about to react so strongly, it was still this paradigm which was directly responsible for the enormous productivity of the Behaviorist school, in all its various branches, including applications to psychotherapy in the second half of this century. A strong error (as Aquinas said, and Paul Goodman was fond of quoting, in works to be discussed in the chapters ahead) is always better than a weak truth; and nowhere is this more evident than in scientific research. The Gestalt school, by contrast, claimed to have laid hold of that third thing, a strong truth—with implications which will be discussed below.

THE GESTALT SCHOOL—EARLY WORK

Nevertheless, in retrospect Wertheimer's original 1912 paper did not depart all that far, if at all, from Associationist principles. True, he did identify a specific "unitary process'—the Phi factor—

by which individual stimuli were translated, within the subject, into a continuous picture; and to this extent he may be said to have moved from the pure "stimulus-bound" position. But these "unitary processes" were themselves "constructed, in a particular fashion, on the foundation of single excitations" (M. Wertheimer, 1912, author's translation). In other words, Exner's Central Confluence again—a sort of melding (or "short-circuiting," as Wertheimer put it) of individual receptor excitations. That is, the emphasis and the control in perception are still seen here as resting with the external stimuli and their corresponding one-to-one excitations, which then, at a certain level of energy, may themselves "jump track" and mix themselves up, so to speak, in the circuitry of the receptor subject. Again, as with the simpler models of Associationism, this is in many ways a commonsensical kind of view: what I see *is* obviously tied up, in some sort of fairly dependable fashion, with what is "out there" to be seen. Otherwise, how would my world work as well as it does, in a practical sense? I steer, for example, mostly by my eyes; and I rarely fall down, or drive into a tree. Therefore, my nervous system is somehow "taking in" and processing what is "there," more or less—as the Associationists maintain. The question is not whether this is happening, but *how* is this happening. At this point, in 1912, Wertheimer had still not taken a very large step beyond the received Associationist explanation.

Nevertheless, there was a nuance of difference, and around this nuance of a somewhat more complex subject role, at least, in perceptual processes than the prevailing model allowed, a new school of thought and body of work quickly began to coalesce. The young psychologists Wolfgang Kohler and Kurt Koffka jointed forces with Wertheimer, first in Frankfurt and later in Berlin, and together with their students and followers they soon began to pour out a stream of papers, experiments, and argument, all designed to delineate the much greater activity of the "passive" perceiving subject than had previously been considered to be the case, and the subordination of all this activity to certain general principles of organization. Moving beyond the original treatment of perception of continuous motion and the Phi construct, their focus now shifted to the more general question of configuration itself: that is, how is it that we see "things" at all, in the discrete and demarcated fashion that we normally do, out of the visual cacophony of light stimuli that impinge on us the moment we open our eyes? Particularly in marginal (and therefore, it was presumed, illustrative) cases, such as optical illusions, judgment of size and distance, or limited visibility and delineation, how is it that we get the whole impressions of things that we do get out of this bombardment of "elementary" stimuli? In an extremely fruitful paradigmatic shift, Wertheimer's answer was that this is not what happens. It is not, he argued, the "elementary" stimuli that are "taken in" by the perceiving organism at all, but rather the *whole configurations* themselves. That is, in terms of the perceiving organism, the "meaningful whole" *is* the stimulus (M. Wertheimer, 1959). Thus, the famous Gestalt dictum (Koffka, 1935), the whole *precedes* the parts. These whole configurations, or "figures" (to use Ehrenfels's terminology, which was adopted by the Gestalt school), can then be broken down, or analyzed, into subsidiary parts; but these parts themselves have the same characteristics of figure against ground —that is to say, of whole configuration: If they did not, we could not "see" them; this is what "seeing" means. If the whole configuration is broken, or interrupted, or otherwise missing, the subject will tend to see the whole anyway (Kohler, 1922; M. Wertheimer, 1925), or to make moves to supply the missing parts, or will experience measurable tension and subjective frustration. This is the way we are "wired" (to use a later cybernetic imagery); at no time, under normal circumstances, do isolated "elementary" stimuli evoke organized responses from subjects, above the level of the "pure reflex" or twitch (Goldstein, 1940); nor can the "higher," more organized responses be "built up" out of the elementary twitches, all strung together "like beads on a string," in the famous image of the Associationist model (Koffka, 1935). Organization, organized figure, *is* the elementary "building block" of perception, and of the subject's response to the perceptual stimulus. Therefore, it is to that organized figure—its analysis, its properties, its formation and structure and dissolution—that research attention should be directed.

Now it should be mentioned here that it is still left somewhat unclear, at this early point in Gestalt theory, whether the "organized wholes" we are talking about are to be found "in" nature, or "in" the perceiving organism, in the structure of the nervous system itself (or perhaps, as we might more likely say today, in the interaction of these two things). In other words, to anticipate the direction of subsequent Gestalt research (e.g., Lewin, 1926), is it the subject's own *interest*, or some other such subjective urgency, which organizes certain forms, certain figure-ground resolutions, out of a field which is in and of itself more or less infinitely malleable? Or are the perceptual structures themselves, the gestalten we are talking about here, more or less already given in the environment?

To some extent this is a question that Wertheimer himself remained on the fence about for the rest of his life (M. Wertheimer, 1961; Kohler, 1959). Certainly in this early phase in his own research, both Wertheimer and his colleagues tended to focus on the environmental side of this interaction. Thus a great deal of research energy was expended in the effort to delineate, and if possible quantify, the various characteristics and properties of the gestalt or figure-ground process itself. In the process, Wertheimer in particular generated a seemingly endless series of "laws" about the "behavior" of perceptual gestalten themselves. Law of Contiguity, Law of Good Continuation, Law of Internal Homogeneity, as well as principles of brightness, distinctness, unity, boundedness, segregation, even abstract categorization itself (which would seem to be a question for explanation here, and not itself an explanatory principle, after the fashion of the old "mentalistic" constructs discussed above)—all of these were posited at various times, and attempts were made to measure them (Kohler, 1920; Koffka, 1935), in an effort to arrive at quantifiable, predictable rules governing when a given set of "elementary" stimuli *in the environment* would "coalesce" into a perceptual gestalt, and when not. Subsuming all the other principles in Wertheimer's model (Kohler, 1920; Petermann, 1932) was the Law of Praegnanz (from the German, meaning full, developed, pregnant with meaning), which stated simply that the percept tends to take on an organized form, and that that organization will be as "good (i.e., simple, coherent) as possible, under given prevailing environmental conditions" (Koffka, 1935, p. 110). In other words, economy of organization, the most meaning or information, in the simplest structural form. Clearly, the translation of abstractions such as these into objective and quantifiable measurement would constitute a difficult if not insurmountable task.

In retrospect, it must be said that this whole direction of research, which may strike us today as curiously Associationist or even "mentalistic" in spirit, was largely a dead end. In spite of the colorful array of interesting and even surprising perceptual problems which are commonly associated with the name Gestalt today, Wertheimer and his associates never succeeded in achieving those "objective," quantified results which they hoped would raise their psychology to the level of the "hard" sciences (Kohler, 1947; Petermann, 1932). The reason for this failure lay in the tautological nature of the various "laws" and propositions themselves. Take, for example, the overarching Law of Praegnanz, from which the various other laws were supposed to be derivable. In stating that percepts are organized configurations, the Gestalt school was making a generalization on data that was, to a considerable extent at least, qualitatively verifiable. In moving from that statement to the "law" that those configurations will be "as good as prevailing conditions allow," an implicit promise of measurability is added. But what is "good," and what are these "prevailing conditions"? In practice, these terms proved impossible to define experimentally, other than in terms of the outcome itself (i.e., the particular figure-ground resolution actually achieved. That is to say, the dependent variable ("good gestalt"), which should vary, according to the "law," with the independent variable ("prevailing conditions"), could only be defined in terms of those conditions, and vice versa. In intent, "good" was supposed to refer to a state of minimal energy (Kohler, 1920, 1922)—by analogy of course to those preferred states of physical systems on which the early Gestaltists kept hoping to be able to base their own model. In fact, however, this "minimal energy" could only be presumed, not measured, in the outcome—much like the "prevailing conditions" themselves, which had to be assumed to have been such as to yield just exactly those particular figure-ground resolutions which were in fact produced by the subject, and no other ones.

In retrospect too, we may well ask why Wertheimer tended to exclude from consideration the one "prevailing condition"—the subject's own interest, motivation, or need,—that might be most accessible to measurement, as well as offering a definitional way out of the tautological problems with the word *good*. (That is, if "good" could only be related to some goal outcome or need satisfaction of the subject, then it might become definable in terms independent of the other experimental variables, and thus be of more service in the validation of the "laws.") The answer, apparently, was that such a consideration of the subject's own internal state would have struck the early Gestalt school as "vitalistic" (M. Wertheimer, 1925)—as introducing vague and subjective "internal states" as explanatory constructs, in the old way of the Associationist model. And indeed, interest and selective attention had been among those principles adduced by the Associationists (Kohler, 1925; Mueller, 1923) to explain the organization of elementary sensations within the preceiving subject. Furthermore, as Goldstein was later to point out (1939), questions of interest and need do not easily or necessarily come to the fore in conditions of lab experiments in visual perception, where people (or occasionally other lab animals) are simply required to report or react to what they see, generally from deceptive or ambiguous stimuli that have no particular personal urgency for the subjects themselves.

That the act or process of perception, of percept resolution, was itself of some inherent interest or urgency for the subject, was one of the hallmark discoveries of the Gestalt school. But just by that very fact, no doubt the first generation of Gestalt researchers feared that the pure process under study would be distorted or obscured, not clarified, by the admission of too many other "life urgencies," beyond the fascinating and inevitable dance of figure-ground resolution itself, which was after all their own distinctive theoretical contribution. In other words, here again we have a case of the assumptions of the model determining the choice of experimental material and conditions—the findings of which then tend to confirm the original, partly unexamined assumptions in their own terms. However (and pure behaviorists to the contrary), it has never proved possible to construct a very interesting or useful theory of *personality*, of wider human functioning, without recourse to some consideration of the needs or intentions of the subjects in question themselves. Thus it is not surprising that it was in just this neglected area—selective attention, interest, and need—that the next and most fruitful extensions of the developing Gestalt model were to be made; extensions which Wertheimer himself never fully embraced, but which will be central to our discussion below, of the elaboration of the Gestalt perceptual model into the areas of personality theory and psychotherapy.

ELABORATION OF THE WERTHEIMER MODEL

Meanwhile, considerable strides were being made in the general Gestalt campaign to discredit the still-dominant Associationist, or Wundt, school (Petermann, 1932). Take, for example, the seemingly simple question of the subjective perception of color. Now if ever there was going to be an area where pure Associationism could furnish a complete explanation, this would seem to be it. That is, color would seem to be a quality "purely" in the stimulus object if anything is, given standard white illumination. Moreover, light frequency itself is readily measurable by a spectrometer. In the case of whiteness and blackness, the reflection or absorption of light by the stimulus object should likewise be objectively measurable. In other words, we "know" a white object is white by the amount of light given off by it and striking the retina—and likewise for the black object.

However, a whole series of experiments by Katz, Gelb, and others showed that this is not at all the case—or at least, not nearly so straightforwardly the case as the Associationist model would seem to predict (Katz, 1911; Gelb & Goldstein, 1920; discussed in Koffka, 1935). Consider, for example, the series known as the "white tablecloth experiments" (Koffka, 1935, pp. 110 ff., 240 ff). Subjects were shown two different scenes, side by side or in sequence. In one, a table appears with a white tablecloth, and various other objects on and around it. In the other, the scene is the same, only with the substitution of a black tablecloth. Illumination of the two scenes is then modulated so that the amount of light given off by the black tablecloth is actually *greater* than the amount given off by the white tablecloth. In other words, one scene is brightly lit, and the other dimly. And yet, not at all surprisingly, subjects had absolutely no difficulty in identifying that the white tablecloth was indeed white, and the black one black, despite the fact that in terms of the "proximal stimuli" the black one was actually "whiter" than the white one, and vice versa. So much for the pure correspondence of elementary proximal stimuli with their composite percept product. But then what is going on here? How *does* the subject manage to make this "correct" judgment, in apparent defiance of the given stimulus conditions? Obviously, there is some kind of selection and organization of "whole-field" cues at work, whereby a relativistic judgment of whiteness is arrived at by the subject, based on the comparative illumination of various other "reference stimuli" within the same scene. In Koffka's terms at the time (1935, p. 250), the subject is constructing and utilizing a "gestalt" which includes a "color gradient" to form the perceptual *judgment*—an interpretation which is certainly within the "gestalt spirit" of emphasis on perceptual organization, but which seems at the same time to be using the term "gestalt" in a quite different sense from its use up to this time—and with considerably more emphasis on the active selective role of the subject than Wertheimer's model would seem to allow, at that early point.

And indeed, this type of slight or not-so-slight leap, without explanation, is characteristic of the first decade in particular of Gestalt research. Thus it is by no means clear that the original Phi phenomenon—the integration of separate "sensations" into a unified perceptual experience—is the same as the resolution of static visual stimuli in the optical field; nor, for that matter, did the original Phi factor itself seem necessarily to follow from Wertheimer's early stroboscopic experiments, which involved an impression of motion in stimuli that were actually separate and stationary, whereas the Phi phenomenon seemed to refer to the opposite case. By the same token, the selective use, as in the tablecloth experiments, of scattered field cues in reaching a particular perceptual *judgment* is not at all obviously the same process as the one whereby figure simply "stands out" from stationary ground in a visual or auditory field. In all of these cases, certainly, some form or act of organization is clearly involved. What is not so clear is that the form is the same in all cases, or that the terms "figure-ground" can meaningfully stand for them all. This point will become more important in succeeding chapters, as we discuss the further extension of these terms into personality theory and psychotherapy. At the time, however, leaps of this kind went apparently unnoticed by the early Gestaltists, in their attempts to extend the implications of the new paradigm—as well as by their critics, in their corresponding attempts to dismiss the new model altogether (see Goldstein, 1939, and Peterman, 1932, for reviews of later criticism of this early work).

Not that the Associationists did not have an answer to questions like these, of perceptual organization and judgment. As indicated above, the answer, generally speaking, was Experience (or, as we would probably say today, Learning) (see, for example, Koffka, 1915; and Kohler, 1925). No doubt, went the Associationist reply, people do display all these interesting and complex processes; no doubt they do tend to cast pictures into figure and ground, see continuous motion where none is present and vice versa, resolve tricky optical illusions, even make complex judgment calls about color, size, identity, and so forth. But all these are *learned processes* —or the complex second-order elaborations of learned processes (but still built up, presumably, by pure association of contiguous stimuli and receptors)—and thus in no way do they invalidate the basic Associationist position, which is that the perceptual/cognitive experience is ultimately reducible, piece by piece, to the discrete external stimuli. Thus it became very important to the Gestaltists to try to devise experiments that would demonstrate that some complex processes, at least, were "prestructured" or otherwise "contained" in the organism, or inborn, and not purely the result of learning (i.e., not completely reducible to external stimuli). Kohler in particular (1915) became fascinated with this problem, which is by no means easy to resolve empirically. Nevertheless, he came quite close, at least, to doing this, in a series of experiments so ingenious, so exhaustive, and so typically "gestalt" that they are worth reviewing in detail here—and so baffling to psychology in general at the time that they had to be repeated several times over, for the results to be generally accepted in the field (Koffka, 1935).

The problem was this: We all know that things far away will appear smaller—that is, present a smaller retinal image—than the same or similar things close up. Still, by and large we have little or no difficulty in distinguishing, by a series of environmental and internal cues (including, for example, sharpness and parallax angle), which ones really are larger, and which merely closer, and even by about how much in many cases (a Gestalt problem of the fourth type outlined above). Furthermore, this ability to make correct judgments about relative size in relation to relative distance is shared by many "lower" animals—even birds, despite their lack of the major supporting cue of bifocal vision. This can easily be shown by training chickens, say, to peck only at the larger of two disks, and then placing the larger disks a considerable distance away from the birds, relative to the smaller ones (i.e., causing the smaller disks to present a much larger retinal image). Generally speaking, the smaller disk has to present a retinal image size something above twenty to thirty times as great as the larger disk before the chickens will start to misjudge, and systematically favor the wrong disk (Koffka, 1935, pp. 85 ff).

Of course, this finding, interesting in itself, could still be the result of learning (and thus conceivably, at least, the result of a purely Associationist process, at least to the extent that any such complex learned behavior could be imagined to be built up in this serial way). What Kohler did was to train three-month-old chicks, who had never been out of their cages, to peck only at the larger disks, and then present them with the experimental situation, under circumstances where they could hardly be imagined to have encountered any similar problem before. True to his prediction, even without any apparent opportunity for previous learning, the chicks showed no systematic difficulty in "knowing" that smaller images, under certain conditions, "meant" larger objects farther away, and vice versa. Moreover, this finding still held, up to size ratios of twenty or thirty times, comparable to those for "experienced" adult chickens (Kohler, 1915). Clearly, either there was some "inborn" organizational process going on here, or else the ability of young chicks to learn this extremely complex judgment behavior on the basis of seemingly negligible experience was so powerful as to indicate an enormous "prepotency" for this particular kind of learning —which comes to about the same thing, as far as the nature/nurture or "prewiring" question is concerned.

To the extent that Gestalt was lined up on the nature side of this dichotomy—with Associationism at the nurture pole, necessarily—Gestalt had "won" the encounter. In the process, it should be noted in retrospect, the dispute and the findings had also moved the Gestalt model itself somewhat further toward the "inner" pole of a somewhat different dichotomy—i.e., the relative emphasis on "inner" versus "outer" factors in gestalt formation— and thus away from Wertheimer's quest for independent, objective, quantifiably measurable criteria of "good gestalt" *in the environment*, where a researcher could get at them. The next contributions to the extension of the Gestalt model, those of Kurt Lewin, were then to take it even further down this same path, and thus further into the realm of personality theory and psychotherapeutic applications, along the lines of development we are tracing here.

THE LEWINIAN MODEL

It was Lewin's contribution, viewed in retrospect, to take the Gestalt model out of the laboratory and into the much more complex realm of everyday life. This development was already foreshadowed, at least, in a highly suggestive early paper, "Kriegslandschaft" ("War Landscape"), written when the author was still on active duty on the German Western Front (Lewin, 1917). The direction of Lewin's argument was as follows: Unless we are experimental psychologists (or lab subjects), we do not actually spend much of our time and problem-solving energy just sitting still making judgments of perceptual scenes, ambiguous or otherwise. Much more common, and more instructive, is the situation in which we *enter* a given field, or are already in motion within a certain environment, parts of which may be in motion as well, with regard to us or to each other. It is our task, then, to use perceptual and other judgments to *negotiate* that field, or move through it, while attempting to reach or accomplish certain objectives, and avoid or stave off certain bad outcomes, along the way.

For example, take the movement of a subject within the war zone itself, where Lewin was actually engaged in the writing of this article (Marrow, 1969). Clearly, in this case the field itself, the whole environment, is taken and used by the subject for much more than a passive or neutral "ground" for the formation of perceptual "figures"—or even a source of cues and clues for complex perceptual judgments on size and color and identity and so forth, though of course all these processes are also going on, at any given time. But beyond this or underlying it, all the entire field or ground itself is organized, prior to the organization of particular figures against it—and organized, in this case, in terms of the dominant prevailing condition of war itself. That is, the perceiving (and moving) subject must resolve the field into a sort of mental/ behavioral *map*, outlining (he hopes) the salient points of safety, danger, shelter, resources, and so forth, *with regard to his own goals in the field.* In our Gestalt terminology, this map, this configuration, is itself a kind of figure, or organized percept, or gestalt— but a figure, certainly, of a new and much more complexly organized kind, against which and *in terms of which* other figures are cast and evaluated. Not just a single bounded "object" or image (whose gestalt properties may be given in the stimuli, *à la* Wertheimer) standing forth against a neutral ground of no momentary interest, but rather a structured and interactive *set* of such "sub-figures," in lively and shifting relationship to each other, to the "ground" around them, and most of all to the subject himself, as he moves or chooses among them. Moreover, it is this figure, this gestalt or map, and not some undifferentiated field, which then serves as the *ground* for various succeeding figures over time— and may in turn be changed by them as they arise or are selected in the field. That is to say, the perceptual gestalten in the "real life" situation do not merely rise and fade and succeed each other in a linear (or Associationist) fashion, as in the lab setting, but actually persist, coexist, and interact in a dynamic and mutually structured way.

For example, take the figure of, say, a haystack, within or against the gestalt or map of the "war landscape." According to the subject's goals of the moment—survival, conquest, escape, reconnaissance, forage, rest, and so forth—the same haystack may be perceived as threat or shelter, protection or obstacle. And more than this: its value and even identity will be perceived differently, according to where and how it lies in relation to other perceived objects on the "map"—lines of sight, battle lines, distance and access, and so on. Thus perceived and located (and thus by definition evaluated/categorized) the haystack becomes part of the changed and organized *ground*, or map, in relation to which new figures may then arise. If the subject is a combatant, the entire field, or map, may be organized directionally—or vectorally, in Lewin's later phrase (Lewin, 1951)—in relation to the opposing vectors of the battlefront, with shifting movements forward and back. If a noncombatant, or a deserter, or a soldier on furlough, or a lover picking his way through the war zone to a rendezvous, the whole field map will be reorganized accordingly, along the lines of his particular needs and goals in each case.

In other words, to use Lewin's later, elegant dictum, *the need organizes the field* (1926). Everything perceived in the field is taken by the subject as either significant or not, in terms of his own needs, and then invested with charge, or value, positive or negative, depending on its perceived status as a potential help or hindrance in the satisfaction of those needs. Subsidiary goals and figures are then further organized with reference to "higher-order" goals and other figures—with the "highest" or most elaborated gestalt being that of the map itself, or "topology" of the resolved field (Lewin, 1935). Resolved, again, in terms of the subject's overarching goal or goals in the field.

The war example is of course in some ways extreme, but very much the same analysis can be applied to more everyday-life situations. Take the case of a student entering college as a freshman. His goals may be ill-defined or various, but let us say he has some clear goal, a clear felt need—to graduate in four years, say, perhaps with a good enough record to be accepted in graduate school at a particular level of competitiveness. His "map" of the campus that results, in part, from this goal will then be entirely different from the "map" of another student whose goals are more relational or convivial—or perhaps political, or artistic, or criminal, or purely scholarly, and so forth. Each of them may be said to be going to quite a different "school," within certain limits placed on their respective "maps" by features and constraints of the "objective" environment. Furthermore, as Goldstein's subsequent work would seem to suggest (1940), each subject will have, above all, the higher-order problem of the *relation of one need to another,* one perceived and valued environmental feature to another, and of all of the interacting needs and features, among each other, with changing valences over time. (The term "valence" itself, with its evocation of the "hard" sciences, is the common translation and was accepted by Lewin himself [1935]; however, a direct translation of the original term, *"Aufforderungsqualitaeten,"* or "demand characteristics," seems to convey better the flavor of the dynamic, interactive interplay between subject, figure, and field, or between higher and lower orders of gestalt formation in the Lewinian model.)

Now all of this, while possibly measurable, is still subjectivism with a vengeance, and of just the type that Wertheimer in particular hoped to avoid, in constructing and extending the Gestalt model (1925; also Sherrill, 1986). If each subject constructs or achieves a different gestalt, a different "map," from the same elements, then the quest to find those reliable, measurable criteria of gestalt formation *in nature* (to use Wertheimer's own terms, 1922, 1925) seems to have been left behind altogther—and with it, the hope of a psychology entirely reducible to physics. Nevertheless, viewed in retrospect this extension of the original model in the direction of the complex interaction between needs and field seems

a natural outgrowth of those increasingly complex research questions, of judgment, choice, and problem-solving (Koffka, 1935), all
of which had already tended to shift the model away from its earlier
emphasis on external environmental or stimulus criteria. At the
same time, the new Lewinian model may be used to throw a fresh
light on some of the earlier work under the Gestalt paradigm itself.
Take, for instance, Kohler's work on relative disk size and distance,
using chickens and apes as subjects (1927). In Lewinian terms, we
may make the simple but crucial point that the chick experiments
described at length above make no sense unless we consider that
we are *starting with a hungry chicken,*—because a well-fed chick
will not resolve the immediate perceptual field in terms of larger
or smaller disks, closer *or* farther away. To repeat, in Lewinian
terms, the need organizes the field. A complete Gestalt view of
behavior here, in other words, would have to include knowledge
of salient needs—or, in less subjective terms, of pre-experimental
conditions (in this case, induced hunger). A scared chicken will
organize the situation quite differently, and fail to exhibit the
behavior Kohler was interested in, one way or the other. Likewise
a well-fed chicken, or a thirsty chicken, a brooding chicken, and
so forth.

The difference of emphasis here is not so much a theoretical
contradiction as it is a shift of the discussion from *capacities* to
behavior—a distinction that will be important later on when we
make the argument that the Gestalt psychotherapy model, as
developed by Perls and Goodman, focuses too much on expressive
capacity and too little on the actual organization of the field that
takes place in the subject's life and behavior. Simply speaking,
Kohler is interested in the first of these two terms, and Lewin in
the second. Obviously, all behavior of a subject is made up of
capacities of that subject (including the crucial but theoretically
neglected capacity to organize those capacities); but just as obviously, not all capacities of a subject emerge in the behavior, or
perceptual resolutions, of a given moment—or ever, for that matter.
The question then is the old Gestalt-versus-Associationism one at
a higher level, and being debated now within different wings of
the Gestalt movement itself: namely, can the complex behaviors
(and perceptions) of subjects be assumed to be somehow merely
"built up" of elemental perceptual capacities, or do we not have
to talk about the *organization* of particular capacities, particular
figure-ground resolutions themselves, into higher-order structures?

This was the essence of the argument that Goldstein was to launch against the Associationist model—and against much of the early Gestalt work as well (Goldstein, 1940).

On the other hand, the original generation of Gestaltists were uneasy, to say the least, with these extensions of their own "objective" model into the "real life," subjective arenas of Lewin's and later Goldstein's work—even when they admired the work itself (Koffka, 1935, pp. 345-6). Nonetheless, a complete theory of personality, as well as any model of psychotherapy derived from such a theory, must be able to address "real" behavior, in this sense, and not just the various capacities or "lab behaviors" that may or may not be the "building blocks" of more complex, more demanding behavioral patterns. Or at the very least, if the theory is to be reductionist on this point, it must be clearly shown that the latter do necessarily follow from the former (indeed, a purely internal critique of early Freudian drive theory could be constructed on just this point). This is a point that will be taken up again and again in the chapters below, in the development of the argument that the Goodman/Perls model of psychotherapy, as suggested above, was based entirely too much on just this kind of early Gestalt lab research, and too little on Lewin's and Goldstein's more holistic extensions.

Finally, the Lewinian model has at least two other implications which were important extensions of the more limited "lab Gestalt" approach, and which will have direct consequences in the application of the model to psychotherapy. The first of these has to do with the fact that the "Wertheimer Gestalt" model, like the early Freudian model (and doubtless for the same reasons, of infatuation with the physical sciences), was essentially a tension-reduction model. As such, it is subject to the same kind of criticism for tautological thinking as was outlined for Wertheimer's "laws" above (see also Guntrip, 1971, on the theoretical problems of tension-reduction models). Not only is tension-reduction difficult to define and measure other than in a circular fashion (the end state has to be presumed to be a state of lower tension, by definition), but there is the additional problem that living organisms seem clearly, at times at least, to make moves to increase, not decrease, tension levels (Goldstein, 1940). By substituting the notion of needs-satisfaction for tension-reduction, Lewin removes the empirical contradictions, at least, if not all the argument-in-a-circle problems of the earlier Gestalt approach.

A second implication of Lewin's work has to do with problem-solving itself. In this "mapping and maneuvering" view of life, Lewin is quite close to saying, in effect, that what we commonly think of as problem-solving is not a special case of thinking, but is actually the paradigm of all cognitive activity, including perception itself. We have already seen how the Gestaltists, with considerable success, sought to demonstrate that seemingly simple processes like seeing form, or judging color, were actually quite elaborate resolutions by the subject of complicated stimulus "problems," which might conceivably have a number of different possible "answers" (indeed, the effect of the early work with ambiguous stimuli, which was intended to be the demonstration of "gestalt properties" in the stimuli themselves, was rather to illustrate this subjective latitude instead). But this is almost a complete definition of problem-solving—and becomes an even more useful one if we add the notion, with Lewin, that not all the "solutions" are equal, and that the *criteria for "right" and "wrong" answers are supplied by the various need states of the subjects themselves* (always in interaction, of course, with environmental conditions). Casting this back into Wertheimer's own terms, we might then say that problem-solving, as the basic tendency of the perceiving subject, is the Law of Praegnanz in action—only with needs-satisfaction now supplying the missing criteria for that troublesome term "good" in the earlier formulation. A new generation of Gestalt research, building now on this perspective, then went on to concentrate on the study of problem-solving itself, with emphasis on the related concept of insight, so central to psychotherapeutic work (Koffka, 1935; Kohler, 1940, 1947), and on the "demand character" of interrupted or otherwise unfinished problems and tasks (Zeigarnik, 1927; Ovsiankina, 1976). Both of these research themes were to figure importantly in the Goodman/Perls presentation of the Gestalt model of psychotherapy, to be discussed in Chapter III below.

GOLDSTEIN'S HIERARCHICAL MODEL

A final elaboration of the Gestalt model, from the point of view of development toward personality and psychotherapy theory, was

the contribution of the neurologist Kurt Goldstein (whose lab assistant, for a short time, was the psychiatrist Frederich [later Fritz]
Perls, whose own work will be discussed in Chapter II). Goldstein,
like Lewin and Perls, was at the German front in World War I,
and much of his subsequent research was carried out on brain-
damaged veterans and other war casualties. As Goldstein was to
describe it (1925, 1940), what was distinctive about many of his
"frontal lobe" cases, as opposed to normal subjects, was oftentimes
not the ability or inability to react to this or that stimulus, in the
way of the Associationist model. Rather, in many cases their problem was the inability *not* to react to certain stimuli (such as a
metaphor, or an obvious lie, or a sarcastic remark), which a normal subject would reinterpret, or discount, or simply ignore (in
this connection, see also Sachs, 1986). That is, the brain-damaged
cases, some of them at any rate, were *stimulus-bound*—exactly
along the lines, Goldstein maintained, of subjects as conceived
under the old Associationist or reflex model. What they could not
do was to *organize* their own reactions reliably, in a meaningful,
purposive, interactive way, in the field. This led Goldstein to his
characteristic formulation that, in the normal subject, *behavior is
always organized,* and *always implicates the whole organism.* These
dominant characteristics of behavior, not surprisingly as Goldstein
saw it, do not show up well in tissue experiments, or anaesthetized/
lobotomized lab animals, or even static lab perceptual experiments
in Gestalt—or in frontal lobe patients. Nonetheless, in actual living processes (and in a characteristically Gestalt formulation), it
is the *organization of behavior that controls the parts,* and not the
other way around (1939, 1940).

Using the same argument and the same research, Goldstein
then specifically criticized all drive or tension-reduction theories,
as considering only these behavioral "parts" in isolation, without
reference to the organic whole, the organized sequences at higher
and higher levels to which the "individual behaviors" are subsidiary.
That is, if a given behavior, normally speaking, can be suspended,
reorganized, or otherwise subsumed in the service of organization
toward a larger goal, then it does not make sense to speak of a
"drive" or "instinct" for that behavior—at least, not in the usual
sense, of a pattern of behavior following on specific internal or
environmental cues, and always following in the same sequence,
on presentation of those cues (see also Hilgard & Bower, 1966,
for a related critique of "instinct theory" in human behavior). Nor

is tension-reduction itself, he argued, a meaingful "drive" or goal of the organism at all, other than in states of deprivation which are themselves pathological. The only "drive" or instinct of which one can usefully speak, in human behavior, is the drive to interact with the environment itself, to exercise the capacities of the subject system—and to organize that interaction into patterns where one behavioral sequence depends on another (and compare here Winnicott's proposition that the only instinct is the instinct for social contact, quoted in Guntrip, 1971).

This drive Goldstein called the drive for "self-actualization," with all the other pseudodrives and behaviors of the organism subsumed within or under it, in interactive hierarchical fashion (1939, pp. 197ff). Maslow later took this model over directly from Goldstein, with credit (Maslow, 1954), together with Goldstein's categorization of subsidiary motivation into "deficiency needs" and "growth needs." Both the psychodynamic and the Associationist models, in Goldstein's view, were built up by generalizing only from the "deficiency needs" or deprivational, reflex states of the organism, without taking into account the overall organizing function of the organism as a whole, or "self," which to Goldstein was the meaningful "gestalt" or organized ground of behavior (1939, pp. 369ff). Both then neglect the crucial issue of organization, which controls behavior in the normal case, outside of extreme deprivational states.

GESTALT PERSONALITY THEORY

At this point, with the work of Lewin and Goldstein, we have arrived at a coherent, ambitious "field theory" of personality in general, with clear implications, at the very least, for cognitive, affective, relational—and psychotherapeutic—domains. The point is worth emphasizing, not because the later Gestalt therapy model drew directly on this personality theory, but because, curiously enough, it did not. Moreover, some later writers have claimed (see for example Fantz, 1975; and Barlow, 1981) that it was Fritz Perls who made the first extensions of the original perceptual Gestalt model of figure and ground resolution into the affective, personality-theory, and even psychotherapeutic realms; and Perls himself (1969b, 1973) gives the reader this impression, at least. This is simply not the case. A quick examination of titles alone should be enough to demonstrate the point: see for example Kohler's *The Place of Value in a World of Facts*, 1938; Koffka's chapters on ego, emotion, memory, and will, 1935; Lewin's *Dynamic Theory of Personality*, 1935; Goldstein's *Human Nature in the Light of Psychopathology*, 1940; and even Wertheimer's "Some Problems in the Theory of Ethics," 1935; or especially Goldstein's "The Organismic Approach to Psychotherapy," 1974.

Every system, as Erikson has observed, has its utopia: every personality theory, by this token, its ideal and criteria of health and dysfunction. These criteria in turn will serve for the derivation of a psychotherapeutic approach, based on that model. This approach may still leave room for the invention of method appropriate to theory; but even here, methodological choice will be considerably constrained, at least, by the terms of the theory of development of health and dysfunction. In the chapters to follow, it will be argued that the Goodman/Perls model of Gestalt therapy, by distorting some parts and ignoring others of this later Gestalt personality model, unnecessarily impoverished its own theoretical base and development—with predictable results in some of the characteristic excesses associated with this therapeutic school. The application of the Lewin and Goldstein models, together with the revisions that then follow in the area of resistance theory in particular, will then be offered as a corrective to some of these problems.

A GESTALT MODEL OF CHANGE

Finally, there is in the Gestalt model, particularly in its elaborations by Lewin and Goldstein, an implicit if unarticulated theory of change and change induction, which likewise has potential applications for psychotherapy and other change-oriented interventions. This flows from the Gestalt view of action itself, and the relation of action to cognition and affect—a problem which much absorbed the early Gestalt school, especially Wertheimer (see

discussion in Koffka, 1935, especially chaps. VIII and IX). The problem, as Wertheimer approached it, had to do with the "mind-body"
dichotomy, which has a philosophical pedigree going back at least
to Plato. That is, either "mind" and "body" (or the material world)
are somehow made out of the same kind of "stuff"—or they are
not. If they are not, then how is it that they seem to "work" on
each other, in both directions, "mind" seemingly making decisions
which lead to physical action, and, correspondingly, the physical
world impinging on mental states, attitudes, feelings, choices, and
so forth? On the other hand, if they are the same kind of "stuff,"
what is this common or commensurate substance, or energy?
Where do we find it, and what are its properties—most of all, its
seeming capacity to take on two such differently appearing forms
as "body" and "mind" themselves? As with his attempts to quantify gestalt properties in nature, it must be said that Wertheimer,
like others before him, did not get very far with this problem. Nor
is Kohler's proposition in this regard—of an "isomorphism" between "mind" (and brain) and "nature"—much more than an
elaborate begging of the question, since the simple assertion of
a structural parallel between the two separate realms, questionable
in itself, still would not explain their interaction (see Koffka, 1935;
Petermann, 1932, chap. III).

Nevertheless, without resolving this age-old debate, the Gestalt
model still throws a useful new light on the cognition/action problem, and in the process answers some questions left over from the
psychodynamic model, which psychoanalytic theory itself has
sometimes had difficulty in explaining. Take the case of the Lewinian "field," with a moving subject negotiating the various perceived
obstacles and resources on his way to some subjective goal by
means of a gestalt "map" representing his own best guess of the
optimal resolution of the two realms, the "inner" world of needs
(and resources) and the "outer" world of resources (and demands).
In this interactive view, every action on the part of the subject
is, in part at least, a *reaction* to perceived field conditions, seen
in the light of one's own valuation of those features, in relation
to one's goals. An approach, an avoidance, a transaction, a resistance, an attempt at influence or environmental modification—
each possible action is an adjustment by the subject, in relation
to his own felt needs and goals, and to the "map" he has constructed, and is constructing continuously. But clearly, if you

somehow change this map, you will get a correspondingly different adjustment, a different course of action on the part of the subject. That is, the model suggests that the most efficient point at which to influence subject behavior is the *map itself*. To attempt to change behavior directly—whether by coercion or some more positive manipulation—would seem likely to generate a great deal more resistance on the part of the subject, who naturally does not wish to walk into any perceived landmines or skip over any rewarding way-stations that still appear ("correctly" or not) on his map. And the more significant the behavior in question, the more resistant we might expect the subject to be. That is, as with Goldstein's critique of early reflex and perceptual work, we might expect *in the lab* that a "pure behavioral" approach to change induction would show positive and consistent results—since in a sense, in the lab there is nothing at stake. But under the more complex and demanding, perhaps threatening, conditions of "real life," these conditioning effects would tend to be disregarded unless they took into account the subject's own topological map of risks, stakes, and rewards—which is to say, his own perceptual/evaluative understanding of the field, in which the conditioned behavior was supposedly to be displayed. Again, if Goldstein is correct, the *organization* of the subject's behavior and world would simply override the training effects, in many cases at least, of a purely behavioral approach. (Of course, there is really no such thing as a "purely behavioral approach," as Gestalt theory itself should demonstrate. That is, there is no way, in the course of influencing a subject's behavior "directly," through reinforcement contingencies, to be sure that the subject himself is not also reorganizing his own "map" at the same time, in the light of these new experiences, as he goes along. On the contrary, by this view we may be quite sure that he is doing exactly that.)

To put the same thing in non-Lewinian language (but still Gestalt terms), we could say it this way: The subject, by definition, always tends toward some optimum state of dynamic equilibrium in the environment (whether this involves tension-reduction or tension-augmentation, as the case may be). This is merely another way of saying it will tend to meet its own needs. This equilibrium, the "best possible under the prevailing conditions," depends on the dynamic relationship (or the subject's own perception of the dynamic relationship) between his own needs and his perceptual resolution of the field—i.e., his "gestalt." That "gestalt" is in turn an "organized configuration of awareness" (Koffka, 1935). Action in the field is then, as outlined above, a reaction, or an adjustment, to correct some imbalance between perceived needs and perceived field conditions/gestalt/structured awareness. But then act to alter that *awareness*, and you will change the resultant action, since the action, in the end, was reactive to the awareness itself. Again, the most efficient "pressure point" for change induction, in psychotherapy or elsewhere, would seem to be not the action, not the behavior in question itself, but the awareness. (Even "structural" or directive therapies recognize this crucial point, since their intention is that the directed new behavior should change the perceived value or expected consequences of such behavior— which is to say, the ground or "awareness map." Obviously, behavioral change which did not have this organizing or "mapping" effect *in the ground* would be a one-time thing.)

Awareness, almost by definition, is never complete; in a sense, that is what the Gestalt model is all about. In the first place, selection has taken place, with possible important elements or features of the field left out or not brought to the fore. In the second place, the process or act of organization itself, by the subject, has changed the relative "values" of the various features, even among those included for notice. To change any of these "elements"—by focusing on neglected areas, bringing new information to bear, reevaluating the "valence" of various elements of the picture, or changing the relationship among them—is to change the awareness, the configural resolution itself, thereby opening, again, the possibility of a different behavior, in adjustment to that changed subjective reality.

Some of this may seem to belabor the obvious, but all the same it is very far from the various coercive, hortatory, or prescriptive approaches that have probably characterized most change induction efforts down through history—and doubtless much psychoanalytic practice, if not theory, down through its history as well (see Bergler, 1956, for a representative sample of the "interpretation as blunt instrument" approach that flourished in at least some psychoanalytic centers around the time Goodman and Perls were writing). It has to be remembered, in the discussion in the chapters to follow of some of the omissions and distortions in the model put forward by Goodman and Perls in 1951, that this was the psychotherapeutic climate they were reacting against.

At the same time, this "commonsense" model goes a long way toward explaining psychoanalysis itself, to itself, as well as to us. That is, Freud's methodology of psychotherapy is heavily based on interpretation—i.e., on the reorganization of established structures, in the subject, of thinking and feeling and approaching other people (and not at all on Associationist psychology, as Perls was later to claim. Perls was evidently misled by the term "free" association," which is of course not conceived of as "free" at all in the Freudian model, but rather as dynamically, not merely associatively, related to the problem structures in question, the "too-rigid" gestalten of the patient's mental life). But the Freudians themselves have had some difficulty in explaining exactly how it is that interpreting a thing makes a difference in the life of the patient. The Gestalt answer is this: any perception, any "view of things," *is* an interpretation of the field, with various accompanying adjustments (actions) which follow, by subjective logic, from that interpretation. The therapist's interpretation (or more properly speaking, reinterpretation), to the extent that it is entertained by the patient, *reorganizes the field*—or at least "destructures" (in the Gestalt term) the existing picture, making a new resolution and a new resultant action both possible and necessary. Thus for example people and situations formerly seen by the patient as threatening, say, may now be seen as neutral or even attractive—a reorganization of valences, in Lewinian terms, with obvious consequences for action. And so on for other, similar examples, all of them common phenomena, certainly, both in psychotherapy and in everyday life.

But the model of change we are drawing out of the Gestalt perceptual model here can go even further than this. Since it is the very nature of the perceiving organism to interpret—i.e., to synthesize the parts, resolve the parts of the field into an organized whole—the supplying of readymade interpretations to the subject by the therapist (or other change agent) may not be necessary, may even be counterproductive, depending on the nature of the particular change being sought. Mere concentration of attention, by or with the subject, especially on some parts of the field that are characteristically out of awareness, will by definition produce some reorganization of the field—and the potential, at least, for a corresponding behavioral change, of one kind or another. The last phrase is significant, because it seems likely that change induction by this approach may tend to be more client-controlled than with some other, more prescriptive methods—less normative, from the change agent's point of view. By contrast, in a more directly persuasive or action-oriented approach, the subject's control may well be expected to center more around resistance—to the particular change desired, to the change agent specifically, or to the whole process. Of course, in an "awareness" approach the change agent may still influence the direction or topic of change in various ways (first of all, by determination or co-determination of the particular unaware areas to be attended to). Still, we might expect that the ensuing behavioral response will be unpredictable, to a greater degree than other models may allow for (which is not necessarily to say a greater degree than the other models in fact achieve).

This approach to change induction, still without full acknowledgment of its theoretical roots in the Lewinian model in particular, came to be known, somewhat illogically, as the "paradoxical theory of change" (Beisser, 1970). Illogically, because there is really no paradox here—as there is, for example, in the phrase "paradoxical injunction," in use in family therapy, where the hope is to induce the subject to do the opposite of what the change agent explicitly enjoins. In terms of the model here, there is no paradox involved in the choice to focus on awareness itself, as a way of influencing action, since that is where action is seen as originating, and thus where it is seen as being most directly subject to influence. All the same, the implications for psychotherapeutic practice are obvious, and far-reaching. Not only is the role of awareness per se heightened, and that of interpretation correspondingly diminished, but the particular processes selected for attention and analysis will differ from those associated with traditional psychotherapeutic models. That is, if it is the nature of the organism to meet and coordinate its needs by the resolution of meaningful configurations, gestalten in the field, then any dysfunction in that process itself will clearly produce other, secondary dysfunctions in all the other processes of life. Thus it is to the *structure of experience* (to use Goodman's 1951 term) that the psychotherapist turns his attention, as the key to health and dysfunction—and to cure.

Again, it is Perls who is generally given credit (and who gives himself credit; 1969b) for developing this application of the Gestalt model, this approach to the psychotherapeutic process. However, sources agree (From, 1978; Davidove, 1985; Glasgow, 1971) that this application was at least in large part the contribution of Paul

Goodman, whose work will be examined in detail in Chapter III. Perls's concerns, and his awareness, were actually quite differently focused. It is to these concerns, particularly as expressed in the only lengthy theoretical statement Perls was to author in his lifetime, that we turn our attention now.

II

The Early Work of Perls

I N 1947 the British publishing house of Allen and Unwin, which had a long-standing interest in psychoanalytical issues, brought out a new theoretical work, written some five years earlier in Johannesberg, by the German-born analyst Frederich (Fritz, later Frederick) Perls, soon to be of New York. Perls at the time was a member in good standing of the various relevant psychoanalytic societies; and under the rather cumbersome title *Ego, Hunger and Aggression* , the original edition carried the subtitle, "A Revision of Freud's Theory and Method." Rambling and disorganized in the extreme ("sketchy" was the author's own word for it, years later; 1969b), the book nevertheless sounded the themes which were to preoccupy Perls for the remaining twenty-five years or so of his life: the central importance of oral and digestive processes, as opposed to sexual, as the controlling metaphors of psychological life; an accompanying positive reevaluation of aggression as part of the oral/digestive process; an insistence on an extreme self-reliance as the absolute criterion of mental health; a relative shift in emphasis (in common with many revisionist trends in psycho-analysis at the time) from past to present; and an extension of Freud's use of opposites or polarities as a key to neurosis. A largely unintegrated compendium of sharp clinical insights, vague philo-sophical musings, and self-aggrandizement in the Freudian man-ner, the book attracted little critical attention (L. Perls, 1982), and soon passed out of print, only to enjoy a surprising and curious subsequent publishing history. Reissued some twenty-two years later, at the height of the author's new prominence as an *eminence grise* of the human potential movement—and without the backward-looking Freudian subtitle, which was now replaced by "The Beginnings of Gestalt Therapy"—the volume quickly took its place for a time on movement bookshelves, alongside other obligatory (and perhaps equally unread) works by authors such as Marcuse, Ilich, Fromm, and even Heidegger and Sartre. Heady company indeed for a work which would certainly be no more than a tiny footnote, at most, in the history of psychoanalysis, were it not for the author's association, in 1951, with Paul Goodman's ex-position of a genuinely new approach to psychotherapy, in Volume II of *Gestalt Therapy: Excitement and Growth in the Human Personality.*

Nevertheless, and despite the revised subtitle, the connection between this relatively early work and the Gestalt psychology which preceded it—or, for that matter, the Gestalt psychotherapy which followed it—was not centrally important or obvious. And this is despite the fact too that the author's three announced intentions at the outset of the book all have a decidedly "Gestalt" flavor: (a) "to replace the psychological by an organismic concept"; (b) "to replace associationist-psychology by gestalt-psychology"; and (c) "to apply differential thinking, based upon S. Friedlaender's 'Creative Indifference' " (F. Perls, 1947, p. 14). An examination of each of these propositions in turn will throw light on Perls's understand-ing of Gestalt psychology at the time, which will then serve to il-luminate certain characteristic themes and problems of the Gestalt psychotherapeutic model to follow.

(a) *"To replace the psychological by an organismic concept."*

First and last, here and elsewhere, when Perls says "organismic," he means "body." Perls himself had been in analysis for a time in the 1920s with Wilhelm Reich, and was much influenced, then and throughout his life, by the Reichian notions of "character analysis" based on muscular tensions and "body armor" (see F. Perls, 1969b, 1971; Reich, 1949). Indeed, when Perls speaks of "holism" and the holistic approach, he generally does not mean, as the Gestaltists did, the organism-and-environment field (Arnheim, 1959), nor does he use the terms as Lewin and Goldstein in particular used them, meaning the organism in its "life space," including environment, overall goals, and the dynamic interaction of all these things (Goldstein, 1939; Marrow, 1969), but rather, again, the *organism as body*. The distinction is an important one, and like many of Perls's particular emphases, one that was to figure prominently in a major split between different "schools" of Gestalt therapy in later years (Latner, 1983; Miller, 1981). For Perls, by and large, the *context* of individual behavior, the particular relevant ground against which the figure of behavior is organized and understood, *is the body*. Curiously, this perspective serves to heighten the very mind-body split he wishes to eradicate or transcend (1947, Part I, chap. 2), while at the same time isolating the "organism," ironically, from the environment as a whole. That is, if body is the (neglected) ground against which thinking takes place as figure, then the dynamic tension of behavior is located *within* the organism, between the two systems or poles of body and mind, even if these poles are seen as endpoints on a related continuum, rather than between the *organism as a whole*, on the one hand, and the environmental field, organized in terms of the organism's needs, as Goldstein and Lewin both would have it, on the other. Thus from the beginning in Perls, a Freudian sense of isolation of organism from environment, self from the social world, pervades his thinking. This too was to be in direct opposition, a few years later, to the Aristotelian, community-directed emphasis of the social philosopher Paul Goodman—and was to persist as an unresolved tension in the Gestalt model up to the present time (see e.g. Crocker, 1983).

In this way too, Perls was to remain all his life the faithful disciple of Reich, more than of any other mentor or precursor—and with many of the same theoretical problems and limitations. That is, Reich's own theory (1949) is by way of direct if only partially acknowledged derivation from the very early, instinct-based Freud—the Freud, for example, of "Three Contributions to the Theory of Sexuality" (1910), or "The Wolf-Man" (1914)—and as such is subject to the same general critique of instinct or drive theory as was offered first by Goldstein (1939, 1940), and discussed in the previous chapter. (It could well be argued that the split between Freud and Reich arose, in its theoretical aspects at any rate, from the fact that far from apostasizing, as Freud liked to claim [Roazen, 1976], Reich's offense was rather in remaining all too faithful to the implications of the earlier, "pure-instinct" Freud after Freud himself had moved on to a somewhat more interactional or "Gestalt" point of view. For discussion of the "two Freuds" in this sense, see also Guntrip, 1971.) Despite reference to Goldstein in connection with the "whole functioning" of the organism (1947, pp. 20, 26), and despite his own work as a lab assistant to Goldstein in the twenties, Perls does not seem to have appreciated fully that when Goldstein speaks of a "whole-organismic" approach (1939, pp. 240, 249), he is referring not just to the psychosomatic whole, but to the whole configuration of the subject's needs and goals in relation to the environment and to each other—to the dynamic *organization* of behavior, not merely its somatic aspect or expression. Nor does Perls seem at all aware, here or later (1973), of the crucial work of Lewin in understanding motivation in terms of the "whole field"—including Lewin's emphasis on the "here and now" (1936), and the "demand quality" of unfinished situations (Zeigarnik, 1927), both of which are topics in Perls's 1947 book, and both of which were to be principal themes of his demonstration sessions in the fifties and sixties (F. Perls, 1969a). Perls does make a single reference to Lewin in the book (p. 101), in which he misattributes the work of Lewin's student Zeigarnik to Lewin himself with regard to the question of "unfinished business." However, topological psychology (Lewin, 1936), which is the extension of the Gestalt perceptual model into motivational psychology, is nowhere mentioned. In view of Laura Perls's and others' description of Perls's work and reading habits, it seems unlikely that he had encountered Lewin's work at first hand (L. Perls, 1982).

(b) "To replace association-psychology by gestalt-psychology."

Perhaps most perplexing of all, in a book full of false starts and nonsequential arguments, is the fact that after this initial and rather sweeping declaration of intent, the word "gestalt" hardly appears in the remainder of the text, and nowhere with any importance or explication of its possible relation to psychotherapy. Thus the question of what exactly the author means or understands, at this point, by the term "gestalt-psychology" itself (or for that matter "association-psychology"), or how it is that he plans to go about effecting the "replacement," is left largely unanswered. Goodman was later to charge that Freud was significantly hampered by an "inadequate theory of awareness" (F. Perls, Hefferline & Goodman, 1951, pp 276 ff.)—that is, by not having access to a Gestalt model of structured awareness, and to the dynamics of that model. In the context, what he was referring to was clearly the heavy emphasis, amounting to almost a sole reliance, on received interpretations from the therapist, along the lines of our critique in discussion of change theory in the previous chapter. Perls offers no such elaboration here, of any connection between a Gestalt theory of awareness and the role of interpretation in therapy. On the contrary, his own reliance on therapist interpretations, as far as the case examples in this book indicate, is completely in harmony with established psychoanalytic practice of the time (with only the *content* of some of the interpretations changed, from libidinal to oral themes).

Indeed, whatever the defects of "Freud's theory and method," to which Perls's book is directed as a critique, it hardly seems reasonable to tax them with being "associationist" in the usual sense at all. Frequency and contiguity, for example, the twin cardinal pillars of Associationist explanatory propositions, play next to no role in Freud's system at all, which is all based on the *structural* importance of certain singular or characteristic developmental events. "Like beads on a string," the Associationists are charged with having regarded the structure of percepts (Koffka, 1935, pp. 588-9): a description more unlike the Freudian organization of memory, for example, could hardly be imagined, with its Byzantine mental topography of peaks and depths, visible and invisible realms, and tripartite warring domains, each with its own attacks and defenses, ruses and strategies, shifting alliances and compromises with the other two powers (and all of it so curiously like the political structure of nineteenth-century *Mitteleuropa* in the post-Metternich age of Freud's own youth, with its three great powers, its famous balance-of-power diplomacy, and its chronic internal tensions. For typical Freudian imagery along these lines, of the tragically fragmented mature personality, see for example A. Freud, 1937). As discussed above, it may be that Perls was misled by the term "free association" in psychoanalytic literature and practice. It is true that "association," or structural similarity (not mere contiguity) plays a role in this therapeutic tool or method; however, what the associated memory material is a key to is a "complex" (Freud, 1985, pp. 37 ff; also 1938, pp. 181 ff.), or internal structure, and not at all another randomly contiguous "unit," as Associationism would seem to have it. In other words, what is called into question here is not only Perls's understanding of Gestalt psychology per se, which is sketchy at best, but his grasp of Associationism and actually of psychoanalysis itself.

(c) "To apply differential thinking, based upon S. Friedlaender's 'Creative Indifference.'"

Salamo Friedlaendler (1871-1946) was a relatively obscure, now almost totally forgotten critic, poet, Nietzsche scholar, and sometime satirical novelist (under the pen name Mynona) of the late Second Empire period in Germany. In his 1918 work *Schoepferische Indifferenz* (never translated, but better rendered in English as "creative undifferentiation," or perhaps "predifference," not "indifference," with its English connotation of lack of investment), he argued, *à la* Nietzsche, for a relativization of descriptive or evaluative terms on the basis of an essentially Aristotelian notion of polar continua in perception (see for example MacIntyre, 1981). Thus the quality "good," say, is not fixed or absolute in value, but rather depends for its meaning on an implicit presumption of "better" than something else—which is itself relative to some corresponding polar term, in this case "bad." This is in explicit contrast, of course, to the Judeo/Christian model criticized by Nietzsche (1886)—or for that matter the Platonic model—under which the notions "good" and "bad," while possibly relative in application, each derive from separate absolutes, to which they refer, and which are given from some source outside the perceptual process itself.

To Perls, the main implication and fascination of this thesis, which was of course quite current at the time, lay in this relativization of "good" and "bad," to standards wholly within the individual organism—which is to say, body. Here again he shows resemblances to the quite early Freud ("The therapist is the ally of the Id;" Reiff, 1962), but without Freud's deep resignation on the matter of the necessity of individual submission to the dictates of society. On the contrary, Perls argues here, the Oedipal crisis, so-called, far from being a necessary step in the internalization of social standards, is rather an instance of the neurotic reaction he calls "introjection"—the "swallowing whole," without proper chewing, of something foreign to the true nature of the organism (Part II, chaps. IV & V). The only true standard, again, is the body. By the actual physical reactions—hunger, taste, disgust, regurgitation, and so forth—the person will establish his own values, his own morality, by "organismic regulation" (Part I, chap. III). As for the question of relationship, or harmony, or congruence, or even membership in any wider social context than the individual body, in Perls's system it simply doesn't come up. Here again we see the seeds of the social or moral solipsism, much more pronounced in Perls's later work (1969a, 1969b, 1973), with which the Gestalt model has frequently been taxed in later years. (And contrast this view, for example, with Goldstein's elegant and richly suggestive 1939 dictum on the same subject: "The existence of one man implies the existence of others.")

At the same time, and almost of more interest than Perls's use of this familiar notion of relativization and polarization in perceptual/evaluative terms, is his curious ascription of its source. This idea, as mentioned above, was in extremely wide and common currency when Perls was a young psychiatrist, in the immediate postwar period. Nietzsche, for instance, was at his popular height in the twenties before being somewhat tarnished by the ease with which the Nazis were able to appropriate and exploit his work. Yet Nietzsche is mentioned only once in Perls's book, and then only in passing (p. 57). Even more glaringly, the idea of "creative pre-difference" or "pre-differentiation" would seem to flow directly from the terms of the Gestalt perceptual model itself, where the "pre-different" stage of thinking or perceiving is the initial contact with the undifferentiated field, before its resolution by the subject into configuration, figure-ground, or a Lewinian "map." In the same way, the ultimate polarization, by this model, or casting of the undifferentiated, preperceptual field into dynamic structure, is the paired polar construct of figure/ground itself: What I see is defined, bounded, and thereby inextricably associated, just as Freud said, with what I do not see or attend to at the moment— i.e., the ground (or in Freudian terms, the unconscious, which is here a special case of fixed ground, bounded off and not available for figure formation). Thus the importance and the intimate connection, as Freud held without ever giving a clear theoretical reason for it, of *opposites* in mental life. (And thus once again a case of the Gestalt model explaining psychoanalysis to itself.) Here again, Perls fails to make the obvious connection—either to Freud, or to Nietzsche, or to the Gestalt model itself (and for a later restatement of his supposed debt to Friedlaender on this score, see also Perls, 1969b, unpaginated).

This peculiar habit, of ignoring an obvious source in favor of an obscure one, is illustrated again in Perls's treatment of the concept of "holism" itself—the doctrine of consideration of the "whole situation" or field in understanding any particular, seemingly isolated phenomenon (1947, p. 7). This approach Perls attributes, again, not to Gestalt in general, or to Goldstein or Lewin in particular, but to Field Marshal Jan Smuts (pp. 28-9; see also Smuts, 1926). At this point it is hard to escape the impression that Perls's insistence on intellectual debts to such relatively obscure figures (intellectually obscure; Smuts was of course politically quite prominent), paradoxically, is in the service of throwing his own contribution, his own originality, into relief. Clearly, if one has derived some interesting notion from a neglected or quite unlikely source, and then applied it far from the area of the source, one's own role and contribution are much more significant than if one simply took the same notion, all readymade, as it were, and applied it right there in the same area. In other words, the smaller debt conceals the larger. It is not conceivable, for example, that Perls, however little he may have read in the field of Gestalt by his own account (1969b, unpaginated; Rosenblatt, 1980), could have been unaware of the obvious emphasis, both in Goldstein and in the earlier Gestalt model, on the whole-field approach, which was absolutely central to a whole generation of Gestalt perceptual work, well-known and much-debated at the time. The same goes for the centrality of the "pre-differentiated" state in perception, in the Gestalt model. By ignoring the roots of these ideas in Gestalt psychology, he is implying (to the lay or medical reader) that he thought them up himself (and note his claim, put forward in 1947 but contradicted in 1969, that he has done "considerable scientific and detailed experimental work" in the field)—or at the very least, that he authored their application to personality theory. Here again, in this regard Perls shows a curious resemblance to Freud himself, whose own resistance to acknowledging any influence whatever (other than the most remote and unlikely, and therefore the most creative) was legendary (Roazen, 1971). On the other hand, Perls was comparatively free of Freud's deep need to control his own "school" and method. If some followers have aped the least useful aspects of Perls's work (in terms of the argument developed here), this has been largely their own doing (Latner, 1985). By contrast, and speaking for a different "school" of Perls's own students, are the remarks of Sonia March Nevis: "We honor Fritz Perls most by emulating that part of him which was critical, creative, and resistant to received ideas" (1979).

So much for the announced intentions of the book. But what then were the foundations of Perls's "critique of Freud's theory and method"—if all the stated aims of the work are either irrelevant, misinformed, or mentioned once and never referred to again? The answer, first and foremost, is *oral aggression*. Perls's wife, Lore (later Laura) Perls, had worked for a time with infants with feeding disorders, and both of them became quite taken with the idea of eating, of the "oral instinct," as a metaphor or prototype of relationship between organism and environment (1947, pp. 107 ff.)—not derivative, as in the Freudian model, from the libidinal/sexual process, but as an equal, separate "instinct" in its own right. (Indeed, in Perls's view there are literally hundreds of other instincts besides the sexual/libidinal [1947, p. 35]; Freud's libidinal model, quite correct in its treatment of the "sex urge" per se [1947, p. 81], errs only in trying to subsume all the other instincts under the rubric of libido itself—which is to say, it is wrong only in its most central and all-pervasive tenet.)

Aggression, on the other hand (and practically alone among the major aspects of life, by this argument), is not an instinct at all, as Freud (somewhat later) would have it, but rather a natural feature or aspect of the activity of *eating*. That is to say, there can be no feeding, no digestion and assimilation and *use* of food by the organism, without a natural and necessary process of *destruction* a breaking down of the food itself to some simpler state more assimilable by the body. This breaking down, of which the prototypical activity is chewing, is oral or dental aggression (Part III, chap. III). *Contact* with the environment, which is necessary for the survival of the organism (and here we see a flavor, at least, of the Gestalt model), is essentially and by definition this process of *chewing* (pp. 107 ff.) By the same token, neurosis or defense (the two terms are essentially interchangeable here, as they are structurally parallel in Freud) is essentially a disturbance in this basic, natural contact activity of *chewing food*. Thus aggression, in this view, far from being such a negative thing (much less a "death instinct" set against the libidinal "life instinct"; Freud, 1923), is equivalent to contact, which is to say it is the natural, essential condition of the organism in relation to its environment (Part II, chap. III). And thereby with a stroke the tragic element of the Freudian model, the picture of man inherently, inevitably at war with himself and his society, is completely erased in the Perlsian view of things. Society may well be inimical to individual expression—indeed, all neurosis is due to "social overcontrol" (p. 224), but no underlying tragic split in human nature itself prevents the complete resolution of the problem, theoretically at least, through psychotherapy (or, potentially, social action). All that is required is that the patient regain his blocked ability—literally, physically—to *masticate thoroughly*, to exercise his dental aggression fully and appropriately, like an independent, self-regulating adult, rather than swallowing things whole, like a nursing baby. And thus the model is melioristic, whatever else we may say about it, to a degree far beyond the bounds of Freud's dominant pessimism—a feature of it, no doubt, which was to appeal powerfully to the social meliorist in Paul Goodman, as we will be discussing in the next chapter.

These defenses, or *resistances* to contact (Part II, chap. II), while theoretically unlimited as in the Freudian model (see A. Freud, 1937), are basically four in number: repression, introjection, projection, and retroflection. Unlike the Freudian defenses, however, which are a logically parallel series of possible responses to various instinctual vissicitudes, here the resistances are all structurally related to each other. All are basically derivative of the fundamental contact disturbance of *introjection*, and all flow, fundamentally, from the same traumatic cause: *too-early, forced or harsh weaning, at the moment the infant passes into the biteling stage*—i.e., at the first eruption of teeth (Part I, chap. VIII; Part II, chap. III). The harsher the mother's reaction (to being cannibalized by the young toothling), the more severe the neurotic consequences (pp. 108–9); however, maternal self-preservation instincts being what they are, it is hard to see how a certain element of neurosis could be altogether missing in even the smoothest course of development—at least provisionally, pending psychotherapy.

Introjection, the fundamental neurotic disturbance or resistance, is natural and normal to the first, suckling, dependent stage of life. In this period of total passivity, the infant merely "accepts" the food that is poured into him, in liquid form, without aggressive activity on his part. All that is required of the infant at this passive stage of development is the "hanging-on bite" (p. 108); the environment (i.e., the mother) does the rest. (One has to wonder here whether Perls ever actually observed a nursing baby, or felt, against his own finger or nipple, the furiously, vigorously aggressive activity of the "passive" infant in this process, especially when no milk is forthcoming.) At this point, one cannot yet speak of *contact* per se, between infant and environment, since the definitional activity of chewing, of breaking down the contacted material, is only minimally present (as for example in the activity of the stomach acids in the digestive process; pp. 107–11). Real contact, between the developing subject and the environment, begins at the teething stage, which unfortunately (as mentioned above) means the infant's attempt to *eat* the breast (p. 108). This in turn, again, leads to the mother's reaction of outrage, punishment, or (worst of all) sudden weaning. Thus, the first experience of contact, in development, is inherently conflictual, and automatically results in a greater or lesser degree of personal rejection—which can be overcome, in later life, only by an absolute and exaggerated *self-reliance*, to recover from the wound (see also 1969b, unpaginated). In Freudian terms, we would call this a reaction formation, a denial-through-overcompensation. Here and for the remainder of Perls's life, it is instead the very touchstone of health and maturity (see for example 1973, p. 47). (But contrast Lewin's remarks on the same subject: ". . . the 'self-made' man, . . . 'standing on his own feet,' . . . [is] as tragic a picture as the initiative-destroying dependence on a benevolent despot. We all need continuous help from each other. This type of interdependence is the greatest challenge to the maturity of individual and group functioning" [quoted in Marrow, 1969, p. 226]. The word "interdependence," needless to say, does not appear in Perls's 1947 work.)

Thus too, as with Freud, we see in the Perlsian model a reflection of a personal developmental issue writ large, or projected as the general human case. In Freud we had the case of the ambitious, aggressive boy, with a powerful mother and a hapless father, who is humiliated by the father's weakness and lack of success (for instance, by his father's humble submission to anti-Semitic threats; see Freud, 1900; also Schur, 1965). Out of his guilt over his desire to surpass or even punish his father, he seizes on the Oedipus myth not merely as the metaphor for one dynamic aspect of development, but as the single, universal, quite literal, and all-determining crisis in the life of the child. In parallel fashion, if less elegantly, Perls generalizes from his own experience of abrupt weaning, and his lifelong struggle with feelings of rejection (see 1969b, unpaginated; also L. Perls, 1982), and projects this as the universal, inevitable developmental course.

What is left out, in both cases, is nothing less than the whole relational context, the Lewinian *ground,* in which these gestures or crises take place. That is, if rejection (or exaggerated competition with the father) is the relational context already, then certainly any experience of abrupt weaning (or of father's weakness) may indeed be interpreted/experienced by the child along Perlsian lines (or Freudian, as the case may be). But it does not necessarily follow from this that the particular issue in question in each case, however potentially universal it may be, will necessarily dominate and color all subsequent development in every case, as Perls (and Freud) imagined. Differing relational contexts will give these and other issues and crises differing meaning and weight, in different cases. That is, to extend a Lewinian or Goldsteinian analysis of the point, the meaning of any figure, any gesture, can never be found in the figure alone, but rather *in its relationship with the field*—which is to say, in the structured ground. We have already seen how Goldstein criticized the early Gestalt and the Associationist models as being "stimulus-bound"—or, in our terms here, "figure-bound," ignoring the crucial issue of organization of the field. Here we can see how the same criticism may be leveled against Perls: he sees the organism (for all his Gestalt claims) as fundamentally separated from environment; he sees health in terms of a rigid and reactive independence from others; and thus he will naturally tend toward an analysis of experience which is episodic and serial/impulsive, as opposed to integrative and sustained—one which focuses on figure alone rather than figure-in-ground. Neither the Goldsteinian notion of a *dynamic hierarchy of figures,* nor the complementary Lewinian view of a *dynamically structured ground,* has found its way into the Perlsian model. The unfortunate consequences of this oversimplified view of Gestalt psychology (and of life) on the development of the Gestalt therapy model to follow will be discussed in the chapters below.

At the same time, and without seeming to be fully aware of it himself, Perls does introduce an interesting and potentially useful shift in the handling of the "resistances" or defenses here, as contrasted with the Freudian model. With Freud (1894, 1920), resistance is always first and foremost a matter of *resistance to therapy* (and thus to the therapist, which comes to the same thing, since in the Freudian model the therapist is always right; see A. Freud, 1937). The "defenses," when they become elaborated, as by Anna Freud, are likewise defenses against instinct—i.e., against the overwhelming and unmanageable pressures of the Id, which are the content of the therapist's interpretations; thus, once again defense against instinct and resistance to therapy become the same thing. With Perls, by contrast, the resistance is not necessarily to the therapist or the therapeutic process or content, but to *contact itself.* In the chapters to follow, it will be argued here that this formulation is inherently inadequate, and contradictory to the fundamental structure of the Gestalt model, in psychology as in psychotherapy. Nevertheless, the shift away from a purely authoritative/adversarial therapeutic stance, in the direction of a Gestalt/interactive view of personality and psychotherapy, is significant and promising. That Perls himself did not seem to realize the implications of what he was saying here is suggested by his assertion at this point that there is no need for him to discuss repression at any length, since it has already been dealt with by "classical psychoanalysis" (pp. 220–1). It has, but from quite a different angle, and with potentially different implications.

The remaining "resistances," projection and retroflection, are likewise developmentally derivative of the basic introjection pattern (which itself was caused, to repeat, by the punishment the infant received when he tried to leave this babyish contact strategy behind and move on to appropriate, mature chewing). With the introduction of authority, at the punitive/weaning stage, comes the split between self and the world—which otherwise would be meaningfully, aggressively, contactfully connected by the chewing function, now so sadly inhibited (pp. 146 ff). This in turn opens the door for *projection*—the assignment of organismic functions, like authority, aggression, morality, and so forth, to the "outside" world, when they should properly be located within the independent organism; and to *retroflection*—an interesting term which Perls evidently coined himself, meaning the turning against oneself, of aggression (or possibly libido) properly directed outward (p. 221). A final "resistance to contact, *confluence*, is mentioned here but not yet classified with the "main resistances" (as it will be in the 1951 collaboration with Goodman). Confluence is the failure to differentiate the self from the environment—a suppression of self to avoid, again, aggressive chewing contact. As with the others, this one is again basically a consequence of introjection, the original disturbance of contact from which all the other distortions and interruptions flow.

The treatment for all these neuroses/disturbances/resistances to contact is simple and straightforward: the patient must regain the ability to *chew*—quite literally,—to contact the environment aggressively, independently, through the exercise of the atrophied dental aggression function. Not interpretation alone, but *chewing exercises* are indicated and prescribed. (In true Freudian manner, the reader is cautioned that the degree of his desire to resist or denigrate this prescription is the exact degree of his own neurosis! p. 192). Once again, Perls is following Reich here, in his emphasis on the basis of neurosis *in the body* and the consequent need for some kind of direct bodily exercise or manipulation as part of the cure. As with Reich, this dictates a certain shift from past to present emphasis in the therapeutic exchange itself: whatever the historical/developmental roots of the problem, this chewing disorder, and the "chewing cure," have to lie in the present. And finally, as with Reich, Perls stresses the focusing of attention on the muscular tension, or block, or inhibition itself, alongside the interpretations, as a therapeutic activity. This focused attention Perls calls, at this point, "concentration therapy," adopting the term directly, and with credit, from Reich (F. Perls, 1947, Part III, especially chaps. I, II, & III). This then is the "revision to Freud's . . . method" which Perls promised at the outset of the book. In place of "free association," which Perls characterizes as a scattershot, random, or "flight of ideas" approach (p. 189), Perls would ask the patient to take up a meditation-like state of focused attention, of heightened *awareness* toward the absent or inhibited or perhaps exaggerated function in question—meaning generally aggression. Again, this may well be based on a misunderstanding of the concept of "free association," and certainly this concentration of attention on the material of analysis is a natural effect of traditional psychoanalysis as well. What is different here is that Perls is giving relatively more weight to that focusing of awareness *as a curative intervention* in itself, apart from interpretation, than it would occur to Freud to give.

But this is highly reminiscent of the Gestalt or awareness-based change model which we said could be derived from Lewin's work on mapping and field-resolution, and discussed at some length in Chapter I. Misunderstanding of psychoanalysis or not, this extremely fruitful methodological shift is actually a fresh extension of Reich's approach—and not merely an application of it, as Perls believes at this point (see Reich, 1949, for comparison). That it is also directly derivative of the later Gestalt model, Perls of course gives no indication of realizing. Here, as elsewhere, he simply does not develop the connection, for all that he has appropriated the Gestalt name. Nevertheless, in his intuitive, unsystematic way, he has apparently gathered a good deal more from his and his wife's work with Goldstein, and from his general exposure to Gestalt ideas "in the air," than he himself can see or articulate. Despite his failure to make good on his announced intentions at the outset of the book, there is here a real step toward a fully "gestalt" model of psychotherapy—i.e., a therapy based on analysis of the *structure of contact*, between self and environment, and by extension within the self as well, among various subsystems of thought, feeling, or action. This budding model, and this application, were then developed further in the years that followed by a small study group that formed around Perls and his wife in New York toward the end of the 1940s (Shapiro, 1985), and then were presented formally by Paul Goodman in 1951 in Volume II of the collaborative book *Gestalt Therapy: Excitement and Growth in the Human Personal-*

ity, a work which extended these "beginnings of Gestalt therapy" made by Perls in his earlier book, and at the same time remained bound by some of the limitations and misconceptions of Perls's own oversimplification of the Gestalt psychological model. It is to these extensions, and these problems, that we will turn our attention in the next chapter.

CHAPTER III

Gestalt Therapy:
The Goodman/Perls Model

Experience occurs at the boundary between the organism and the environment, primarily the skin surface and the other organs of sensory and motor response. Experience is the function of this boundary, and psychologically what is real are the "whole" configurations of this functioning, some meaning achieved, some action completed. The wholes of experience do not include "everything," but they are definite unified structures; and psychologically everything else, including the very notions of an organism or an environment, is an abstraction or a possible construction or a potentiality occurring in this experience as a hint of some other experience. We speak of the organism contacting the environment, but it is the contact that is the simplest and first reality . . .

The human organism/environment is, of course, not only physical but social. So in any humane study, such as human physiology, psychology, or psychotherapy, we must speak of a field in which at least social-cultural, animal, and physical factors interact. Our approach in this book is "unitary" in the sense that we try in a detailed way to consider *every* problem as occurring in a social-animal-physical field . . .

On reflection, the foregoing two sections must seem obvious and certainly not extraordinary. They assert (1) that experience is ultimately contact, the functioning of the boundary of the organism and its environment, and (2) that every human function is an interaction in an organism/environment field, socio-cultural, animal, physical . . .

. . . psychology studies the operation of the contact-boundary in the organism/environment field. This is a peculiar subject-matter, and it is easy to understand why psychologists have always found it difficult to delimit their subject . . .

That is, the contact-boundary—for example, the sensitive skin—is not so much a part of the "organism" as it is essentially *the organ of a particular relation of the organism and the environment*. Primarily, as we shall soon try to show, this particular relation is *growth* . . . (Perls et al., 1951, pp. 269–70).

5 8

To READ Paul Goodman, even briefly, is to step into a different intellectual world—a world at once denser and more sweeping, faster-paced as it rushes by you, and everywhere charged, in the Lewinian sense, beyond the normal urgencies and valences of theoretical discourse. As with Erikson in a different sense, a certain seductiveness of style, a seamlessness of the whole, almost works against analysis of the parts. *Does* experience really occur "at" the surface of the skin and "other organs of sensory and motor response?" In what sense? Or is it not something I synthesize myself, in a place difficult to specify, but at any rate quite far from my "sensitive skin?" Are the "meaningful wholes" of my reality really reducible, in this sense, to physical contact? Is this intended as a metaphor, or as literal description? Almost before we can pose the questions, we are already being assured that all these points, after all, are really "obvious," and nothing at all controversial has yet been said. Does this mean that we, the readers, are not quite in a position to comprehend the obvious, without considerable effort? If so, what hope do we have of digesting the remainder of the book, when subtle or controversial issues begin to be raised?

Both Laura Perls and Isadore From (the two living deans of Gestalt therapy, both members of the original study group which Goodman's manuscript grew out of) have maintained that this density of style, this insistent consequentiality so characteristic of Goodman's work in general (and so utterly different from Perls's), make it impossible to "introject" the Gestalt model—i.e., to take it in uncritically, in the Perlsian metaphor, and "swallow it whole" (Wysong & Rosenfeld, 1982). On the contrary, from the record it seems more likely that the opposite is the case. The complete absence, in the extensive Gestalt therapy literature of the past thirty-five years or so, of any systematic critical assessment of Goodman's work would seem to indicate that it has been very difficult, at best, for students of Gestalt to do anything *but* take the Goodman/Perls model uncritically, as an undigested whole—or else, as is no doubt more commonly the case, to ignore it completely (either by encapsulation or by "spitting it out" as something "inedible," to continue the Perlsian imagery). If experience is "ultimately" a matter of sensory and motor domains, of interaction between "organism and environment," then what are we to make of "internal" experiences? And how does all this differ, after all, from an essentially Associationist, "stimulus-bound" model? Above all, if psychology is the study of this interaction "at the boundary," what do we call the process and study of the *organization* of these interactions—which would seem to be another order of activity, at least, and one taking place somewhere other than the surface of the skin?

On the other hand, if it is the meaningful "wholes" that are "real," does this not imply that the subjective *organization* of interaction, of contact in the everyday sense of the word, is the important thing after all; and does this not in turn contradict, in emphasis at least, the assertions of the immediately previous sentences? In other words, is there not still an unresolved tension here between "early" and "late" (i.e., Goldstein/Lewinian) Gestalt models embedded in Goodman's view from the start, yet unexamined either by him or by subsequent writers? Here again, the very authoritativeness of tone, the high impenetrability of style in Goodman's exposition may work against easy analysis of questions of this kind. All the same, this type of analysis—this "destructuring," to use the Gestalt term—is our present task.

Contact, according to Goodman, is "the awareness of, and behavior toward, the assimilable novelty; and the rejection of the unassimilable novelty" (p. 270). We can taste (so to speak) the Perlsian flavor in this formulation, but clearly the original Perls notion of contact is extended here considerably beyond mere chewing. By adding "awareness" to "behavior," Goodman takes the definition firmly in a more "Gestalt," less Reichian direction. In other words, contact, as here defined, involves a kind of *judgment*, an internal process of problem-solving—like the Lewinian Gestalt definition of awareness itself. Therefore, contact (like Gestalt awareness) is by definition "creative and dynamic . . . it must cope with the novel, for only the novel is nourishing" (p. 271). Thus, further extending the analogy between contact and problem-solving, "all contact is creative adjustment of the organism and environment"—i.e., growth, or change. "Aware response," by the same token, *is* growth—which is in turn the "function of the contact boundary," i.e., the fulcrum point of nourishment and change (p. 271).

Therefore, by an algebraic substitution of terms, "psychology is the study of creative adjustments." Abnormal psychology, it then follows, "is the study of the interruption . . . of creative adjustment"

(p. 271). And thus we have already spent a good page, at least, in discussion of a few salient points from considerably less than a page of Goodman's prose. At the same time, by a series of dazzling and seemingly effortless leaps, we find ourselves light years away from the Freudian model (or the Perlsian, for that matter). "Creativity [contact] and adjustment are polar" (pp. 271-2): i.e., adjustment alone will not be the underlying criterion of health here, as in the Freudian model (at least in Goodman's view). On the contrary, this (and not the substitution of oral for libidinal "instincts") will be the foundation of *Goodman's* critique of Freud: that Freud, in his conservative resignation, requires the adjustment of the individual to the (quite flawed) social order, to the neglect of the naturally, inherently radical/creative activity of the organism, in contacting/assimilating/changing its own environment—and itself (pp. 448 ff). In other words, the basic nature of the person does not lie in his irrational, animal impulses, which must be channeled for survival, as the overriding problem of life. Rather, human nature is to be found in the *process of contact* itself, with the environment (including the social environment). And that contact process, we have already seen, is inherently of the nature of a new problem to be solved at every moment, and thus of excitement (meaning energy for the new), growth, change. (As for libido versus peristalsis, Goodman's natural imagery, like Freud's, is unfailingly erotic, just as Perls's is instinctively digestive; see chaps. XII & XIII).

Obviously (as Goodman would say), we have the materials at hand at this point for a new definition of therapy, and of health and dysfunction—and possibly a new methodology of therapy as well, all deriving in some way from this notion of contact as "creative adjustment." The idea of "creative adjustment," or "aware response," would seem to include the original Gestalt idea of awareness as a structured process of judgment or problem resolution, the Lewinian extension of a meeting or approach in a field which is dynamically structured in relation to the subject's needs (to seek out and touch the new), and possibly Goldstein's notion of a dynamic hierarchy of gestalten as well (since growth equals self-actualization)—and to add to all this the further dimension of a dynamic *exchange*, something transacted, created, incorporated, given birth to, that was not there before. All this is a rich and promising therapeutic prospect indeed, and seems to open up the

vista at last of a psychotherapy that can talk about the real processes and issues of life—decisions, choices, commitments, losses,
priorities, investments, disappointments, values, goals, desires passionate or calculated, and how we long and strive to weave all these
disparate strands together, and to do justice to them all (and to
ourselves)—yet without reducing all these terms of living down
to some other elementary particles and drives which fail to cap-
ture the *whole* of things (in the way of psychoanalysis, or Associationist psychology, reducing complex processes to component parts
which, when recombined, do not seem to yield the original experiences again).

That is, as we go through life, encountering the new (as Goodman says) in large transactions or small, we take in the environment, change it, assimilate it, move on—and are ourselves changed
by the encounter, in ways perhaps influenced but still not entirely
controlled by our various early experiences, of weaning, or libidinal
rivalries, or chewing habits, or behavioral schedules. The process,
just as Goodman is suggesting here, is more creative than that,
and at the same more unpredictable—and much more of a self-
directing feedback loop, where the next step can never be entirely
predetermined until the previous one has been taken, and the
results of that one are in. Thus our conditioning, neuroses, values
(introjected or otherwise), commitments, overall goals may be laid
down in a relatively stable fashion, and may well determine subsequent experience to a point, but that experience in turn will then
act upon all those prior determinants, dynamically and reciprocally,
as the process goes along. Which is to say, with Lewin, that it is
the new dynamic *organization* of all these things at each moment
that is the "cause" of present behavior. In the same way, overarching goals may yield subsidiary, instrumental needs; but then
in the course of satisfying these second-order goals, the original,
determining urgencies may themselves be changed, or reevaluated,
or forgotten. When people criticize psychotherapy, as they have
been doing for nearly a century now, as being divorced from "real
life," it is generally antireductionist and interactional issues of this
kind, in some sense, that they have in mind. Here at last, one begins
to think, might be a therapeutic approach that is so experiential,
so phenomenological, as to address these issues of the *organization* of experience, of the choices and relationships among different
felt urgencies, directly—instead of atomistically/reductively, in

terms of some supposed underpinnings, or drives, or building blocks of behavior. All this seems the promise of Goodman's beautiful oxymoron, "creative adjustment," seen against the background of his view of an organism in dynamic exchange with the environment, and the whole development of the Gestalt field model of personality up to this time.

Thus the disappointment, when it comes, is all the greater. Contact, we are told (p. 272), is not the creative resolution of the whole dynamic, interactive flux of needs within the organism, in relation to themselves and at the same time to the resources of the field as given by structured awareness. Rather, it is suddenly something much simpler than this: the forming of a figure of interest against a ground or context of the organism/environment field. A dynamic *selection* of structurally related needs, in relation to their own urgencies and the available resources *may* be involved —or it may not. The therapy, then, "consists in analyzing the internal structure of the actual experience, with whatever degree of contact it has"—not with reference to its living qualities of choice, hope, loss, achievement, but rather with regard to its *gestalt properties*, of unity/disunity, brightness, cohesion and continuity, segregation, boundedness, and so forth (pp. 272–3). In other words, all at once we are back in the early Wertheimer model of gestalt process, where the relevant issues are not the dynamic relations of gestalten among each other, at various levels and urgencies— but the "dynamic relations of the figure and ground" (p. 273). These "gestalt properties"—i.e., the qualities listed above, of "strong figure"—then give nothing less than an "autonomous criterion of the depth and reality of the experience" (i.e., how vivid it is), much as Wertheimer hoped they would (see Chapter I above), if admittedly without his aspirations to lab measurability and quantification of the various "strong gestalt" criteria.

As in the Perlsian model (but unlike the Freudian), healthy functioning and good psychotherapeutic process then tend to become the same thing, for "the achievement of strong gestalt is itself the cure." In other words, no reference to wider or higher levels of organization of gestalten is necessary: given a "strong gestalt" in the moment, all the rest will somehow take care of itself. This is so because the "figure of contact," the strong gestalt, "is not a sign of, but *is itself* the creative integration of experience" (p. 273, emphasis added). By a process of directed awareness, of focusing attention on the weakness or disunity of various areas of the gestalt which is formed at the moment, "it is possible to remake the dynamic relations of figure and ground until the contact is heightened" (i.e., the gestalt becomes a stronger one; p. 273). No doubt this is possible, along the lines of the change-through-awareness model outlined at the end of the first chapter, and discussed again with regard to the early work of Perls. And certainly, as Goodman says here, "awareness is not (just) a thought about the problem but is itself a creative integration of the problem." The only trouble with this formulation is that the problem itself is so narrowly defined. To repeat, not the complex, richly phenomenological Lewinian mapping of the dynamic structure of ground is meant here—nor the Goldsteinian problem of the dynamic interrelations of gestalten of varying orders and perhaps competing urgenices—but the infinitely simpler problem of a single gestalt configuration against an "empty ground" (p. 299). In other words, not the lifelike problem of relative dynamic motivations in relation to the structure of the field, but the old, simplistic "lab" problem of resolution of a *single* figure, by a stationary subject, in an artificially bounded setting (there the lab experiment, here psychotherapy itself.)

It could be, of course, that the more demanding problem of the dynamics of gestalten, in relation to the dynamics of ground, could be built up, associationistically so to speak, out of the atoms of these individual, stationary gestalt "percepts." However, both Lewin and Goldstein, as we have seen, argued persuasively that this was not the case. Goldstein in particular argued that the principles of Gestalt itself would dictate that the whole of organization, the dynamics of gestalten, cannot be generated or derived from its individual gestalten, or parts. As evidence, he cited the cases of some of his brain-damaged veterans, who could achieve "strong gestalt" in the moment, but not the higher-order organization we are talking about here (1939; for a contemporary treatment of the same line of argument, see Rosenblatt, 1988). Organization, as the very essence of Gestalt theory teaches us, is always the new thing, always the "creative adjustment" which cannot be determined or predicted entirely from the given elements themselves, but grows out of the subject's own dynamic approach. Here Goodman, in the very same way as Perls had done previously (and no doubt by direct adoption of that part of the Perlsian model), stops short of that crucial next step—the step of gestalt-formation itself, which brings the model to life and raises it above the level of organization of the trivial, the impulse-ridden, the isolated moment. Gestalt formation, that is, in the wider and deeper sense, of the organization of gestalten or percepts themselves, both within the dynamics of the moment at various levels, and in enduring structures over time.

Thus, in the Gestalt therapy model of 1951, from the very outset, we have a powerful new approach to understanding and changing human behavior, which promises to restore the social, transactional dimension of life so neglected by Freud—and which is at the same time fettered, or impoverished, by a reductionism to overly simple elements, much like the Freudian and behaviorist approaches the new model seeks to improve on and replace.

This limitation of the new approach follows from Goodman's original formulation of terms, which locates the focus of health, dysfunction, and therapeutic intervention in the dynamic tension between *figure* and *ground*—rather than between *gestalt* and *gestalt*, or one order of configuration and another. But as Goldstein pointed out (Gelb & Goldstein, 1918), the essence of behavior, the one "instinct" of the organism, is organization itself. Just as the "elements" of perception are organized interactively by the subject (and not principally "given" in nature, as Wertheimer had it), so these configurations themselves, of figure and ground resolution, are dynamically related *to each other*, with a tension or "demand quality" which is not satisfied until an overarching, hierarchical, or otherwise organized configuration of *gestalten* is achieved (see Lewin, 1926). It is in this way that Lewin's and Goldstein's perspectives are the same: the organism is not "satisfied," the tension not released, until the *whole field* (including the subjective time dimension) is organized, and the various urgencies related meaningfully *to each other*, and to the field. (Of course, this state of unsatisfaction, or chronic tension, may persist indefinitely, at a cost in "life energy" [Lewin, 1935]; that is, after all, what we mean by neurosis, whether in this model or another.) Certainly, people can and do exhibit disturbances in figure formation per se, along Goodman's lines: this would seem to be the chronic state of the Freudian hysteric, say, unable to form, feel, and own a sexual impulse—or for that matter of any other "neurotic," where the nature of the problem was specifically the

6 5

repression or inhibition of self-expression, particularly the (*partly*) body urges, of sex and aggression ("I have yet to see a case of nervous breakdown which is not due to *overcontrol*"—Perls, 1947, p. 224). But is this the main reason why people come to psychotherapy? Perhaps in 1900, or even 1951, it was. Today, probably more common is the case of the person who suffers from anomie, lack of direction, lack of meaningful goals, lack of *relation* with other people and of one dimension of life to another—and the case where these disorders are not entirely removed just by regaining and expressing the inhibited impulses. Certainly the ability to form *passionate figures of contact* (to use Goodman's elegant phrasing)—whether sexual, aggressive, altruistic, aesthetic, productive, playful, or otherwise—is essential to gaining full functioning. But the achievement of powerfully energized *urges*, however important, does not by itself produce a full, "self-realized" life—as example all around us today amply demonstrate. By concentrating on the urge in isolation, by ignoring the configuration of the *structured ground*, Goodman fails to realize the full antireductionist, anti-isolationist potential of the Gestalt model itself.

What are the reasons for this failure? How is it that Paul Goodman of all people, first and last a social reformer, gave expression to a model that fails to do justice to the organized connections between "organism and environment," which is to say the tissue of social relation—in favor of a more isolated, internal, and episodic process of serial figure formation? First of all, there is the fact that Goodman based his model, in part at least, on Perls's understanding of Gestalt psychology itself. Perls, as we have seen was probably not aware of the later elaborations of the Gestalt model, in the highly phenomenological approach of Lewin and Goldstein (see for example Perls's engaging and disarming autobiography, in which he confesses to not having understood Goldstein's use of the term "self-actualization" for some thirty years or more—or ever, in our view here; 1969b, unpaginated, see fourth page of regular text). Perls's own background was first in medicine, then in psychoanalysis, with particular emphasis on the body theories of Reich. His attraction to the Gestalt model, as we have seen, was probably for the support it seemed to offer, as a "transactional" picture of the organism-in-environment, to his own views about the centrality of feeding and of autonomy. Moreover, viewed in "reaction formation" terms (see Chapter II, above), this reduction of the whole social, personal, relational world to the single, neutral label "environment" would seem to have the effect of reducing the importance of that world, in emotional/relational terms, and making it more manageable (again, see Perls, 1969b, for discussion of this troubling issue in his own life). It is worth noting here that Goodman, perhaps out of discomfort with this effect, repeatedly seeks to emphasize that "environment" does indeed include other people. By further contrast, the Lewin and Goldstein models cut exactly the other way, restoring the social dynamic which has been "reduced out," so to speak, in the earlier, Wertheimer Gestalt model. Perls took what he wanted from Gestalt—and what he understood, which may come to the same thing—and used it, then and later, in the service of elaborating his original themes of *oral aggression*, splits or polarities, "unfinished business" (i.e., blocked aggression), and absolute autonomy of the individual—even when the Gestalt model itself inclined toward an opposite view.

Paul Goodman, for his part, came to Gestalt from an entirely different angle. Goodman was above all a social philosopher and critic (as well as a poet and novelist), grounded in the classics, and committed in every aspect of his life to thoroughgoing social reform (Davidove, 1985). His particular political/philosophical interest was in anarchism as a basis for community (Goodman, 1947, 1966). Not, as in the popular notion, anarchism as anarchy, or random lawlessness, but rather the social/political doctrine, deriving from Proudhon, Bakunin, and Kropotkin, that the spontaneous, self-regulating networks and institutions of individuals, coming together and generating their own living structures out of felt, shared needs, will work more to individual and social advantage than the prescribed institutions of government. Anarchism thus seeks not the abolition of government, but a different, and reduced governmental role, whereby central authority and resources are used primarily to support fluid, spontaneous community structures and programs generated from the "bottom up," not the "top down" (Ilich, 1969). These were the themes Goodman propounded all through his life and work, in a series of novels, stories, plays, poetry, essays, and books of social criticism—and in *Gestalt Therapy: Excitement and Growth in the Human Personality*, Vol. II (which Goodman authored substantially alone, on the basis of a shorter manuscript of Perls; see From, 1978). The book-length essay *Growing Up Ab-*

surd and the semi-autobiographical novel *Making Do,* in particular, were extremely popular and influential with the social-activist generation of the Civil Rights, antiwar, commune, and other parallel movements of the 1960s and 70s (see Goodman, 1947, 1959, 1960, 1962, 1966). Much of this generation, which regarded Goodman as a liberating social prophet, probably had no idea that he had ever involved himself in "mainstream" concerns of psychology and psychotherapy.

The analogies between Goodman's anarchistic social views and his exposition of the Gestalt therapy model here are obvious and important. In both cases, there is a deep faith in the creative power of the untrammeled individual. Just remove the unnecessary strictures (social or neurotic), and the process of "creative adjustment" itself, spontaneous and self-organizing, will do the rest. Indeed, in many cases the social and neurotic fetters may prove to be one and the same: "If the institutions and mores were altered, many a recalcitrant symptom would vanish very suddenly" (p. 276). This is a position with which Freud—particularly the early Freud— would have no difficulty agreeing (Freud, 1985).

For if the argument here is that Goodman neglected the crucial issue of organization above the "figure-bound" level, this is by no means to suggest that he was not deeply concerned with just these questions. If Perls could write a charming and brilliantly artless autobiography at the age of seventy-five without a single reference to his children, his philosophical values, or any social or political commitment whatever—and barely any to his wife, his clients, or any personal friend—Goodman's autobiographical writings are exactly the opposite. Community, courage, commitment, nobility, grace, loyalty, passion, family, love in all its forms—these are the themes and the language of his journals, stories, poems, novels,— and his psychological writing as well (see for example Perls et al., 1951, p. 274). The question is not one of values or commitments (both of which, in the terminology developed here, are stable organized features of *ground*), but rather of different times, different urgencies—which then result in a different organization of the theoretical field. The times against which Goodman (as well as Perls) was writing—say, roughly from the advent of Hitler through the demise of Joseph McCarthy—were, in today's terms, oversocialized and overcontrolled. Not just sexually and materially, but politically, socially, militarily as well—the "institutions and mores" that Goodman refers to. The forty years between Goodman's birth in 1911 and the publication of *Gestalt Therapy* in 1951, on the political level, were an unending procession of war, civil wars, colonial wars, depression and oppression, fascism of the left and the right, more war, genocide, and finally the Orwellian state of continuous militarization of civil life, under a nuclear cloud. Goodman, as an intellectual, an artist, a leftist, a Jew, a professed anarchist, and a sexual libertarian, would have figured on practically every list the fascists of both political extremes have ever devised for the suppression or elimination of "undesirable" social elements. It can hardly have seemed conceivable, in McCarthy's America, that within a single generation there would come a time when social disorder and disorganization would be the order of the day, when age-old barriers of race, gender, political persuasion and even sexual orientation would crumble and fall—for a time, anyway—and the authority of government, church, family, Pentagon, even Freud himself, would be everywhere mocked and flaunted—and all of this with the accompanying alarming effects of an apparent falling off of passionate involvement, self-sacrifice, community and aesthetic standards, and deep commitments of every kind, in place of the spontaneous *increase* in these virtues that Goodman himself would have expected from these social reforms.

In 1950, at the height of the Cold War, by far the more present danger must have seemed the steady march of regimentation and militarism, at the expense of everything in life that was playful, passionate, spontaneous, tender, erotic, authentic—or of life itself. If received authority is false and destructive, then it becomes urgent to find other sources, other standards for establishing what is real and what is worthwhile. Thus the importance of an *autonomous criterion of value* (p. 272). This, as we have seen, Goodman hoped to have found in the spontaneous "organismic" process of gestalt formation itself, safely located within the individual, away from the corrupt bonds of social authority (the state may tell you what to see, but it cannot actually see it for you). And this he built the model on—even at the price of a certain disjointedness, a certain trivialization of the system, which then may come to seem somewhat impulse-bound, "atomized" in its time perspective and social relatedness, or just unable to deal with the larger issues, of therapy and of life.

For Goodman, the larger issues were clearly always there, whether the model was well-adapted to tackle them or not. "Do not be afraid," the authors wrote, "that by dissolving conscience you will become a criminal or an impulsive psychopath. You will be surprised, when you allow *organismic self-regulation* to develop . . . , how the principles *you* ought to live by will seem to emerge from your very bones and will be *obviously appropriate . . ."* (p. 259). Today we might say that Goodman (and Perls) took the positive side of the strong social bond for granted, and that without it, we find it hard to be so sanguine about a shared notion of what is "obviously appropriate." No doubt if Goodman were alive today, he would say much the same thing. At the time, the increasing tyranny of artificial social bonds, imposed from above without regard for the creative autonomy of the individual, must have seemed much the more present danger.

What weapons does the individual have at hand in the struggle against these forces? Subversion, imagination, authenticity, sex, comedy—the usual devices of the age-old spirit of anarchism in the struggle for human freedom (p. 295). At the end of *Empire City*, Goodman's massive 1942 allegorical bildungsroman, the hero, Horatio, prepares for battle. Saul's armor, Goodman reminds us, was too heavy for the boy-subversive David:

> Somewhere there is the enemy. What strength and weapons will he have to meet him with?
> Horatio tickets them off on his fingers, the weapons we have that do not weigh one down. First there is the simple sling and shot that hits the booby on the brow. Second, there is the eloquent trumpet that makes the walls fall down. And third, the arrows of desire.
> Also, there is the force that is in the heart of the matter, that, as if stubbornly, makes things exist rather than be mere dreams or wishes. For whatever a thing happens to be, there it is, as we say, "You can twist and turn it but there it is." That's a strong force. It is usually not a violent force, for it urges the smallest possible increment of change, whose lightning-like summation has brought about a change.

Today we live in an age that was brought into being, in part, by the subversive undermining, by Goodman and many others, of dehumanizing "institutions and mores" of previous generations.

70

In the process, things have not gone exactly as he expected. Nevertheless, it is our loss that Goodman is not here today, to mock the false gods of our own era.

All the same, the model Goodman presents, however incomplete by this analysis, still provides a powerful tool for diagnosis and intervention, from quite a different angle from the dominant Freudian model of the time. What are these differences? In Goodman's words, "concentrating on the structure of the actual situation; . . . experimenting; promoting the creative power of the patient to reintegrate the dissociated parts" (p. 278). Again, the emphasis on the "development of the actual experience as giving autonomous criteria . . . not as a clue to some 'unconscious' unknown or symptom, but as the important thing in itself" (p. 279). In other words, the notion of awareness as a structured, creative act which resolves some problem in a "figure of contact" is the theoretical founation; the process of awareness, of gestalt formation itself, is the subject matter; and the heightening, or directing of attention, or focused awareness, is the methodology (p. 282). Still, without fully articulating the connection, Goodman here is drawing on the change model which derives as a consequence from Lewin's "life space" theory, outlined in Chapter I. Neurosis, following Perls here (and also Freud, e.g. 1900) is always of the nature of a split, a loss of some important part of the self, which is disowned (see also Sullivan, 1953), repressed (Freud, 1938), or projected (Perls, 1947), so as to become unavailable to the person in the "urgencies" of living (Perls et al., 1951, pp. 281–2)—that is, in the formation of "figures of contact" with important goals and resources. But then these splits, these distortions, will be apparent in the process of creative awareness, creative adjustment itself—which will be the subject of examination in therapy. If a person characteristically interrupts or inhibits a full "figure of contact"—whether at a certain point of excitement or typically with regard to certain subject matter (sex, aggression, dependency, and so forth) or in the presence of certain feelings—then that interruption will be the area attended to and the subject matter of discussion in therapy. Each act of "creative awareness" is of the nature of a problem to be solved, a new resolution to be achieved: therapy thus takes on the character of an *experiment,* in some new solution, or resolution, of those dynamic tensions. This takes place spontaneously, and is spontaneously different, because the act of focused awareness (on some forbidden or frightening or otherwise blocked-out topic or feeling) has changed the elements to be resolved, and changed the dynamic between them (pp. 290–1; again, this is a process more clearly explained by Lewin than by Goodman and Perls). Thus therapy, in another one of Goodman's elegant oxymorons, is a "safe emergency," a place where dangerous experiments can be undertaken safely (p. 320). (And thus Goodman gives support to the kind of isolated "experiment," or exercise, which is popularly associated with the Gestalt model. This approach, which was ultimately trivailized by Perls [1973], and then raised to a high aesthetic level by Zinker [1977], will be discussed more fully in the next chapter.)

To reiterate: the basic human condition, as with any living organism, is to establish and maintain a nourishing relationship with the environment (to live *in* the environment, Goodman would prefer to say). This is the central problem to be resolved anew, at every moment. The resolution of the problem, at a given moment, *is* contact (of organism and environment), *is* experience, *is* "structured awareness" (since there is no other kind), *is* creative adjustment, *is* growth. All these terms are fundamentally equivalent—which shows both the lingering flavor of the Perls model here, and at the same time how far we have come from those beginnings. The organization of experience "at the contact boundary" is the subject matter of psychology (with the unfortunate caveat here that Goodman limits consideration of this crucial issue to the organization of particular figure-ground resolutions, as discussed above). Likewise, the disturbance of this ongoing, fluid sequence of figure-ground resolutions is the subject matter of abnormal psychology—and of psychotherapy. This model, besides being eloquently presented, is elegant, spare, tightly cohesive, even bright and graceful—all the qualities, in short, that Goodman lists as characterizing "strong figure," or "good gestalt" (p. 272). As such, it resists "destructuring," as we have said—just as Wertheimer said any strong gestalt will do (1922).

The criticism of this model offered here is this: that the process of figure-ground resolution alone cannot be made to carry all the freight Goodman would load onto it, for all the reasons expounded above. Internal as well as boundary processes, the resolution and integration of competing figures, competing needs, and the question of higher and lower orders of organization—and the satisfying placement of all this in a *structured ground*—are also essential to the "meaningful wholes of life," and cannot be completely derived or inferred from the particular figure-ground resolution of the moment. To say the same thing the other way around, the processes of relationship, meaning, and the organization of various needs and gestalten themselves, which are the very things Goodman hopes to address with his new therapy (see for example pp. 294–5), cannot be reduced to the elementary "building blocks" of figure-ground analysis alone. Indeed, when Goodman speaks of "contact," he clearly means something at a much higher level of organization, at least at times, than he is generally willing to speak of directly (p. 305, for example). In his understandable zeal to avoid replacing one authoritarian system with another, he has artificially restricted himself to the use of elements that can be viewed (though this is itself debatable) as "autonomous"—not subject to any standard of judgment outside the individual himself. Ironically, then, "figure-ground" becomes in Goodman's system what "mature genitality" is in Freud's or Erikson's (1951): that single act or process out of which all the rest of life, inferentially, is to be organized, and to which that life can again be reduced, in analysis. Unfortunately (or fortunately), in all these cases, the theoretical price is a simplistic reductionism which cannot be justified—either by the facts of living and clinical work or, in this case, by the terms of the full Gestalt psychological model itself.

But what then of the questions of neurosis, or treatment, or resistance (whether resistance to treatment or resistance to "contact") under this model? First of all, when Goodman speaks of neurosis as "interruptions to contact," he explicitly does not mean all interruptions, all disturbances at the "contact boundary." Any crisis, any emergency may clearly lead to a temporary destruction of "equilibirum" at the boundary, or a "blotting out" of awareness, full or partial (p. 309). At such moments the subject may well be paralyzed, temporarily, from taking the action which normally follows from or "completes" the contact—or he may have to act/react on the basis of guesswork, "hallucination," partial blindness, or some other inhibited awareness. This happens all the time, and does not yet constitute neurosis. Neurosis is a *chronic* state of interruption, or inhibition, in some aspect or subject area of the contact/awareness process (and is by definition "out of awareness," a phrase which Goodman prefers to "unconscious," which seems to suggest that the awareness exists "somewhere else," as the Freudian system would have it; p. 301). The "repetition compulsion," or "return of the repressed" in Freudian terminology, is not the traumatic scene itself, or even the blocked libido "reasserting itself" but rather the natural tendency of the creative awareness process toward resolution, by the natural laws of gestalt formation, seemingly "compulsively" repeated only because the resolution itself is repeatedly blocked. That is, in neurosis not all the elements required to resolve the problem at hand in some potential contact are available, because of awareness blocks (p. 345). Thus, the Goodman model, however hampered by too-close adherence to the simplest case of gestalt formation, nevertheless offers a powerful and powerfully different account of the apparent phenomenon of "repression"—which is, of course, at the core of the Freudian system. In the process, once again we see the Gestalt model explaining the psychoanalytic—and without recourse to all the various anthropomorphic/political constructs and theoretical geography of that complex system.

The therapist, among other things, acts under this new model as an *agent provocateur*. That is, by working with the client to focus awareness on blocked or distorted material or processes, he/she acts to disequilibrate, or *destructure*, the client's own habitual way of looking at things, of organizing experience. In the process, and as a consequence, the new structure, the new "creative adjustment," will emerge spontaneously, by the very nature of the organism: ". . . the self-awareness is an integrative force; . . . from the beginning the patient is an active partner in the work, a trainee in psychotherapy" (p. 293). The therapy is "complete" not when every "complex" is "dissolved," but when the patient has reached "such a point in the technique of self-awareness that [he] can proceed without help" (p. 292).

Of course, these propositions, especially the first ones, are things that therapists of most schools have always subscribed to, with the exception perhaps of the very early Freudian. But here again, it is a particular contribution of the Gestalt model to explain certain processes which various other schools,—particularly the psychodynamic—take for granted. Moreover, it is important to notice here that in our discussion of Goodman's model so far, we have not found it necessary to make any reference to active fantasy, role-play, "body work," or any other of the various "techniques" commonly associated with Gestalt therapy. Under the terms of the theory, the emphasis here is on the *process* of subjective organization (rather than merely the content which is organized), and on the *experiment* (formal or informal) of a different organization, a different "figure of contact" (p. 275). In the course of applying that emphasis, clearly body language, styles or mannerisms of speech, and above all the interpersonal meeting style (with the therapist), as well as content itself, may be scrutinized with a view to picking up blocks, distortions, or contradictions (tensions) in awareness. Similarly, there is no theoretical reason why formal exercises, or experiments, role plays and fantasies and so forth, cannot be used in therapy to experiment with new creative resolutions, which include previously excluded material or feelings. But there is no particular reason either why any or all of these methods, or "techniques," *should* be included in the therapeutic work in order for it to "qualify" as Gestalt therapy. On the contrary, in the succeeding chapters we will have occasion to refer to a variety of Gestalt work which does not make use of any of these "techniques" (beyond the general attention to contradictions in the client's "way of being," including physical manner, which would be common to most therapies),—as well as to some work which relies heavily on therapist-structured exercises and role plays, but which by this analysis is not Gestalt work at all.

But what then is the role of content, or "history," in this model? How does the Goodman Gestalt model regard transference, which is by definition the "living out" of history in the present interaction? The answer sheds light on the Gestalt model—and again on the psychodynamic. Transference, we might say, is the "Trojan horse" of Gestalt (or even of object relations theory) in the citadel of the early psychodynamic model. That is, in Gestalt terms, Freud's great therapeutic insight (which redeems and largely contradicts his early drive model) was that the patient *organizes the felt reality of the present encounter in terms of the felt realities of the past.* In spite of Freud's attempts (e.g., 1923) to explain this process in terms of impersonal libidinal cathexes, the door was nevertheless opened to a much more interactive therapy, in which the therapeutic relationship itself is the lab, so to speak, for experiment in Goodman's sense, in its own terms. Goodman is at his iconoclastic best as he criticizes a certain, easily recognizable brand of psychodynamic work, in contrast to the Gestalt approach:

. . . Rather than being liquidated, they [i.e., defenses and aggressions toward the therapist] are accepted at face value and met accordingly man to man: the therapist, according to his own self-awareness, declines to be bored, intimidated, cajoled, etc.; he meets anger with explanation of the misunderstanding, or sometimes apology, or even anger, according to the truth of the situation; he meets obstruction with impatience in the framework of a larger patience. In this way the unaware can become foreground, so that its structure can be experienced. This is different from "attacking" the aggression when the patient does not feel it, and then, when it has a modicum of felt reality, explaining it away as "negative transference." Is the patient never to have a chance to *exercise* his wrath and stubbornness in the open? [p. 293]

This is the participant-observer role of the psychotherapist—a delicate balance, as therapists know. The emphasis is shifted here toward the therapeutic encounter *as a real relationship,* while still regarding it as a "lab," or microcosm, for the study of the patient's life—"in the framework of a larger patience." The role of transference, and of history in general, is then by no means eliminated, but is in a sense reversed: where in the Freudian model the interaction in therapy is reduced to a commentary on the past, here the past is *adduced,* as a commentary on the difficulties or mysterious aspects of the present, real interaction. At the risk of belaboring this crucial point: this does *not* mean that Gestalt therapy is antihistorical, ahistorical, or just plain uninterested in history. On the contrary, in the terminology of the argument developed throughout this critique, the personal subjective past is part of the *structured ground,* which conditions the dynamic creation of the present figure. It is rather that the past is not regarded as strictly, directly causative, in quite the Freudian sense. Gestalt therapy is not interested in a "rehash" of the past for its own sake, because this is not seen as making a difference (p. 293). The *causes* of present behavior, as Lewin maintained, must be sought in present dynamics (1935). But like dreams, or fantasies, or mannerisms, or the structure of the interaction with the therapist, or "body language" itself—or even "techniques"—the past history of the patient is a clue, a way in to understanding the subjective organization, or organized ground, of his present felt reality.

Now what of the defenses, or "resistances," in all this? Like Freud, Goodman emphasizes that a defense, or "neurotic mechanism," is a *solution* to a problem—though characteristically, Goodman highlights the creative aspect of the problem-solving act, where Freud would use the more pessimistic language of compromise between opposing "forces" (p. 522). The problem in question is a block, or disturbance, in *awareness*: "Neurotic behaviors are creative adjustments of a field in which there are repressions" (p. 522; and note here how Goodman is virtually forced by his own model, in discussing actual life problems, to use the Lewinian language of a structured field, which he otherwise avoids. "Repressions," in this sense, are by definition ongoing structures of ground, enduring over time, across the lives of many momentary figures). Thus, in contrast to Perls, the "neurotic mechanism" here is not so much a "resistance to contact" as it is a *kind* of contact—i.e., the best contact, by the definition of contact itself, that the subject can make under the given circumstances (which is to say, without full relevant awareness, without all the relevant elements of the problem at hand). The distinction (between "resistance to contact" and "kind of contact") is important, and will be developed further in Chapter V below, where it will be argued that the Goodman/Perls model of the "resistances" really derives from Perls as a precipitate (or introject) of psychodynamic theory, and is not fully reconcilable with the terms of the Gestalt model itself. For an example of this unexamined split within Gestalt theory, see for instance pages 163–170 of Volume I of *Gestalt Therapy*, where "resistance" is defined as a withdrawl or refusal to "make contact" (and where a typology of neurosis is given that is quite different from the Goodman account in Volume II of the same book. (Authorship of various sections of *Gestalt Therapy* remains somewhat indeterminate, but it is surely not Goodman who wrote that *"a major problem for all forms of psychotherapy is to motivate the patient to do what needs to be done"* [p. 164]. As the discussion down through this chapter has indicated, nothing could be more foreign to Goodman's thinking than this externally imposed view of motivation and therapy.)

Thus, as with Freud, all neurosis, all contact disturbance, goes back to a *repression*—i.e., a problem in awareness (or what Perls would have called a "scotoma" or blind spot; 1947, p. 65). But the existence of the "blind spot," to Goodman, does not alter the dynamic truth that contact, "creative adjustment," is still taking place, as well as it can (and here the echoes here of Wertheimer's Law of Praegnanz), given the resources and elements that *are* available to the subject at the time. (Complete withdrawal from any interaction whatsoever with the "novel" is a conceivable state, but could not be of long duration, or death would ensue.) On the other hand, Goodman extends the Freudian view of neurosis as a "creative" (or conservative) solution, to all contact moments, all life processes. In Gestalt, not only the symptom or defense, but *every* exchange, every "seeing," every structured awareness is of a problem-solving nature. It is an irony of the Freudian model that only the neurotic is seen as doing something creative with his organization of the world (see for example A. Freud, 1937): thus the close traditional association, in psychoanalysis, between neurosis and art. Goodman, following Rank (1958), would turn this formulation around: in the Gestalt view here, there is no difference between "life" and "art." Life is art—the continual succession of awarenesses, of creative adjustments. To think otherwise would be to fall prey to yet another of the many "neurotic splits" of our culture, in Goodman's view (pp. 310, 342). What we would add to this formulation, in line with the argument developed above, is only that the Goodman model stops short, in this emphasis on the "continual succession" of such creative moments. Rather, as Goldstein maintained, it is the *integration* of such moments into meaningful wholes of a higher organizational order that makes a life—and that therapy must be able to address directly in dealing with health and dysfunction.

Given this view, it is with understandable reluctance (and perhaps some pressure from his coauthors) that Goodman undertakes a typology of neurosis in Volume II at all. When he does, he emphasizes the fluid, unreified nature of the mechanisms in question, by placing them in the context of a structured sequence of contact steps:

(a) CONFLUENCE.

This mechanism, as with Perls, is an overidentification of self with the environment, a failure to perceive and distinguish the *boundary* between the two, by which the organism identifies and knows itself. Thus, excitement, the energy at the boundary for the contact resolution, is diffuse and unlocalized, not brought to bear on the problem as aggressive energy for a new solution. Important parts of the self are desensitized or split off, so that the only possibilities for (partial) satisfaction are in "random spontaneity independent of the ego-surveillance" (p. 528). The prototype disturbance of this order would be the Freudian hysteria, in which scattered and "regressive" behavior is the best contact solution the subject can make, with the severely diminished self-resources at hand. But here again, the "symptoms" and the "neurosis" themselves, however unsatisfying in the long run, are still not "resistances to contact" in the Goodman (or Perlsian) sense presented here, but rather the "best contact," the best resolution of environmental/self resources and subjective needs that the person can make at the time. And here too, increased *awareness* is the necessary and sufficient condition—not for "dissolving the resistance," but for making another contact solution possible. This point, that the Goodman/Perls "resistances" are better conceived as particular contact solutions, is one to which we will return again and again in the argument below.

(b) PROJECTION.

If the excitement develops and is felt (instead of being diffused or disowned, as above), then *emotion* arises (p. 530). Emotion, as Goodman conceives it, is the relationship of *value* between the need and the object—i.e., love, desire, disgust, fear, hatred, longing, and so on. If the interruption to the contact process occurs here—that is, if the emotion is not felt and owned—then projection is the result. That is to say, the emotion is "there," but it is not "mine:" therefore, it must come from the environment. The characteristic stance will be provocative—because of rising to or defending against some imagined approach, aggressive or erotic or otherwise. A typical Freudian character disturbance arising from contact distortion of this type is of course paranoia.

(c) INTROJECTION.

On the other hand, it is possible that the excitement, or energy building for creative adjustment, is interrupted, and the need or "appetite" involved is replaced by some other desire or organizing principle (such as a rule) which is foreign to the organism itself (p. 528). In the Perlsian model (1947), as we have seen, this was the basic case for all "resistance to contact," and followed from the original interruption to healthy dental aggression (whether literal or metaphorical). Here, as mentioned above, Goodman is rather following Freud, not Perls, in making repression—the awareness disturbance itself—the fundamental problem in neurosis. That is, where Perls was unambivalently phobic about any sacrifice of autonomy, any influence whatever from another person or from the community on the individual (conscience, remember, was a neurotic introjection), Goodman is ambivalent, at least, on the same question. Goodman values community, sees it as the natural context for the unfolding of human nature (Goodman, 1947), and indeed is drawn to the Gestalt model in the first place partly because of its firm placing of the individual in a social context, in contrast to Freud. At the same time, as we have seen above, he deeply fears the coercive, deadening power of the collectivity on the spontaneous, creative individual. The partial resolution of this tension for Goodman (and here we can see his attraction to the Perlsian model, as well as to the Freudian and to Gestalt itself) lies in the healthy, positive reevaluation of aggression itself, which Perls espouses. Introjection (like retroflection, below) is fundamentally an inhibition of aggression, a failure to *meet and act upon the new thing*, thereby changing it and making it one's own. The Freudian counterpart would be the obsessive, guilt-ridden, masochistic personality, weighed down by the burden of the punitive superego (the ultimate introject *par excellence*).

(d) RETROFLECTION.

Here Goodman essentially follows Perls, in defining the term which was an original contribution of Perls's aggression model. If the arousal/excitement is felt, and the accompanying emotion (evaluation of the goal in terms of the need) is owned—and no foreign standards or values are substituted for one's own organic needs—then an aggressive stage in the contact process itself must necessarily ensue (p. 531). In Goodman's language, something that is old must be destroyed, manipulated, approached, dissolved, or otherwise modified, in the course of encountering the "novel," so that something new, a new synthesis, can arise. If the aggression at this point is inhibited, or forbidden (by some introject), or otherwise chronically blocked, it must then turn against the only safe object in the field—i.e., the self. This retroflection is the turning inward of energy/aggression which should be directed outward, for the full satisfaction of the need. Failing to make full contact, or aggressive destructuring, with the new, the retroflector "goes over the same material again and again" (p. 532). It is tempting, if irreverent, to conclude here that the Freudian analogue would be the successful analysand himself, at the termination of a classical psychoanalysis: the person who, in the psychoanalytic caricature, understands everything (in the past), and changes nothing—because he chronically breaks the contact process at the moment of *action*, of aggressive acting on the new material or object.

Curiously, Goodman, the apostle of sexual libertarianism, in a sudden and surprising throwback to the *very* early Freud (see 1985, for material from the early 1890s), gives as a prime example of retroflection the act of masturbation, which he likens to rape, assigning the satisfaction to the aggressive/sadistic hand, and seemingly denying the element of erotic pleasure altogether (p. 532). This might be dismissed as an idiosyncratic aside, were it not for the fact that it also points up an unexamined problem with the notion of retroflection itself: namely, what to do with the case of supporting or taking care of the self, rather than seeking that support from the environment. The implication here is that it is always or inherently/potentially neurotic to meet one's own needs from one's own resources, as opposed to seeking satisfaction from outside (a curious and exaggerated reversal of Perls's solipsistic definition of health [1973] as being the transition from environmental supports to self-supports). This in turn goes back to the kind of basic question about the Goodman model we raised at the beginning of this chapter—i.e., whether it makes sense to think of experience as something that happens "at the contact boundary," when so much of what is meaningful, and what is organizing/orienting in life, seems rather to take place in some sense "within" the personal boundary (which is to say, again, at the level of organization of the *ground*, against which Goodman's "figures of contact" stand). Here we see a fundamental ambivalence on the part of Goodman, the artist/intellectual, on the subject of solitude, introspection (which comes off, it must be said, in rather bad odor throughout the book; see especially chap. XI), and the *organization of the self*. This same ambivalence about the dual nature of retroflection itself, and how to value the processes of self-caretaking and self-reflection is carried over in the work of the Cleveland School, which will be examined in the following chapter (see e.g., Polster & Polster, 1973).

(e) EGOTISM.

Finally, if all these various pitfalls are negotiated, and the "meeting" with the new is achieved, there comes the moment where the self must "let go of the self," for the actual contact in the fullest sense to take place (p. 533). That is, the "something old" that must be destructured and reorganized is not only in the environment, but also *in the self*. In Piagetian terms, both assimilation *and* accommodation (the restructuring of the self) must take place (Piaget, 1947). At this point, the self must be "sure enough of itself" to risk itself, its own given, past organization, in the new encounter. If it cannot, the result is "egotism"—the clinging to the frozen *self as it was*, the inability to take the plunge, and risk change, loss, unfamiliarity. Spontaneity is lost, and an exaggerated, hypercautious deliberateness appears.

It is worth emphasizing here that this term, this "neurotic mechanism," is a pure and saving Goodman addition to the Perlsian "resistances." It appears nowhere in Perls's writings, early or late; and in general it is neglected in the Gestalt literature of the succeeding thirty-five years (but for significant exceptions, see any of the writings of S. Nevis, 1981, 1983, 1985a, 1985b, 1986a, 1986b, 1988 in press; also Latner, 1982). That is, for relationship, or community, or commitment to take place, there must be a *giving of the self* to that contact, to that new organization—an element of *loss* (of pure/Perlsian "autonomy")—for the new configuration to be able to arise (see also E. Nevis, 1987). This omission, in much Gestalt writing, is not accidental. Rather, it is a natural consequence of the Perlsian insistence on absolute autonomy, which is at the heart of the excesses and distortions, in this argument, of the "human potential movement"—and of some Gestalt therapy as well. This is the paradox and the irony of the "me decade," of the seventies and eighties, which were so much in the Perls spirit:

namely, that full satisfaction, full contact which nourishes the self and adds to it, cannot be achieved without a certain sacrifice of the purely autonomous self, narrowly conceived—a letting-go of the self-in-isolation, or the self-as-impulse, in favor of direct commitment to *organized structures of ground,* which the Goodman/Perls model has shied away from addressing. But this commitment is the very thing that is inhibited by the Perlsian phobic stance toward any infringement on personal autonomy. Goodman, for his part, remains of two minds to the end, on this crucial theoretical and therapeutic issue.

The Freudian analogue here would of course be anorgasmia, the inability to *let go,* so that (in Goodman's language) the need can be resolved and a new figure can emerge. And indeed, in this egotistical age of repressions dissolved, impulses acted upon, traditional introjects expulsed, we are told that sexual dysfunction is everywhere on the increase once again. Again, it is our loss that Goodman, with his gift for powerful sexual imagery, is not around to teach us the meaning of this disturbance to our most social selves.

The Work of the Cleveland School

THE PUBLICATION in 1951 of *Gestalt Therapy: Excitement and Growth in the Human Personality* by Perls, Hefferline, and Goodman—especially Goodman's theoretical presentation in Volume II—drew considerable interest in the new model from psychotherapists and others looking for alternatives to the often rigid psychoanalytic practice of the time. Out of the original study group that had spawned the book itself, the New York Institute for Gestalt Therapy was established, with a regular discussion group as its main activity, which interested therapists and other visitors could attend. Among these visitors some time in 1952 were several young psychologists from Cleveland, who returned home to found a study group of their own, later importing Perls, Goodman, and other New York Institute members as teachers and visiting therapists. This new group in turn founded the Gestalt Institute of Cleveland, in 1953, which became and has remained the most vigorous and prolific center for publication and training in the field of Gestalt therapy over the ensuing three decades and more. (In part, this predominance of the Cleveland group over the years has been due to the relative failure of the original New York group to publish further in the field. Of the original founding group at the New York Institute, Goodman wrote hardly anything more in the field before his early death in 1971 [see only Goodman, 1977]; Perls concentrated for the rest of his life on the popularization of a particular, idiosyncratic brand of directed psychodrama, lecturing and demonstrating widely but writing very little of a directly theoretical nature; while Laura Perls and Isadore From, mentioned above as the "deans" of Gestalt therapy and both quite influential through their teaching, have both declined so far to publish extensively in the field [see Wysong and Rosenfeld, 1982].)

While the Cleveland group was thus exposed to the teaching of a number of the original New York Institute members, including both Perlses and Paul Goodman, it was Isadore From who quickly became their main outside lecturer, supervisor, and workshop leader—as well as individual therapist to many of the Cleveland group for a number of years. For five years, From traveled from New York to Cleveland twice a month for teaching and therapy. Then, after a hiatus, he resumed these trips on a once-a-month basis for another five years (From, 1982). Not surprisingly, the work of the Cleveland group is very much marked by the influence of From's teaching, which was generally based on the Goodman/Perls model, but showed certain characteristic shifts of emphasis which will be discussed below. From this basis (and with a characteristic tilt toward the Goodman/From perspective and away from Perls), various members of the Cleveland group then made a number of important and fruitful extensions, applications, and modifications of the original 1951 theoretical presentation—in the process often raising but generally not addressing systematically many of the same concerns of the theoretical critique developed in these chapters. These extensions and applications are discussed below:

THE EXPERIENCE CYCLE

In 1947 Perls outlined what he called (characteristically) the "metabolism cycle," consisting of six stages, to describe the "achievement of organismic balance"—i.e., the meeting of a need, always conceived in the Perls model in terms of the prototype activity of eating (p. 69). The six steps or stages were (1) rest—a state of equilibrium (like the early Freudian, as we have seen, the Perlsian model is based squarely on tension-reduction); (2) a "disturbing factor . . . internal or external"—presumably meaning either a need or a threat of some kind; (3) "creation of image or reality"— the meaning of this is unclear, but it does seem to suggest some reorganization of the field for action, though this of course would not be Perls's terminology; (4) "the answer"—that is, contact with the goal (always defined, as we have seen above, as "chewing"); (5) tension reduction, which is self-explanatory, if theoretically debatable; and (6) return to "organismic balance" (p. 45). Health is then equated with "organismic self-regulation" (p. 46)—the smooth functioning of the cycle—which presumably should be no more than a matter of eating when you are hungry, taking only what tastes good to you, and stopping when you've had enough, without interruption or interference from troublesome foreign introjects such as "conscience" (in other words, the same schema we have been criticizing as simplistic throughout this analysis). Dysfunction, or neurosis, is then the interruption of that smooth functioning, which may occur characteristically at any point along the cycle—with the various points of interruption corresponding to the various "resistances to contact," or neurotic types.

As discussed at length above, the specific objection raised here to this model—or this sketch for a model—is not so much that it is wrong, as far as it goes, as that it is subject to a sort of theoretical tunnel vision, an insistence on focusing only on the individual impulse or desire in isolation, which violates the crucial field implications of the Gestalt model itself. Paraphrasing Goldstein's criticism of earlier work, the model is "figure-bound." Invariably, it seems, when reaching for examples to illustrate this sequence, Perls (and other Gestalt writers as well) comes up with "disturbances" which are either trivial (getting a drink of water, brushing a fly off one's face) or heavily biological (defecation is probably Perls's favorite illustrative case)—or both. Occasionally, his illustration may be sexual, but this is much rarer than with Freud or Goodman,—possibly because sexuality resists reduction to the purely physical. The effect is a picture of human life as impulsive, episodic, socially isolated, lacking in temporal continuity and overall organization.

Ironically, in view of Perls's earlier professional history, this model, only slightly caricatured, then resembles nothing so much as one of Goldstein's brain-damaged war casualties (1940), with their intact ability (in some cases) to follow the given urge to completion, but no capacity to handle problems of *organization* of goals, or of their own impulses, which thus remain serial, not in dynamic relation to each other (as a subsidiary goal is dynamically related, for example, to the overall plan of which it is a part). This organizing function is perhaps distantly implicit, only to be skipped over, in Perls's stage three, "creation of image or reality"—a process which, as we have seen in the Lewinian model, involves the organization of the whole field of internal needs and external features into dynamically related, relatively stable, *structured background* configurations for new figure formation. But the point is not developed. On the contrary, any such stable predispositions, or features of the personal ground, would verge dangerously close, for Perls if not for Goodman as well, on fixed or arbitrary standards of conduct and value.

Indeed, the very notion of "personality" would seem, for Perls, to involve rigid structures of ground which may threaten the uninhibited pursuit of the impulse of the moment—which in turn remains the norm of healthy functioning. But as the Lewin and Goldstein models demonstrate, there *is no such thing* as the impulse in isolation, without reference to some consistent, stable organized features of the subjective ground, against which the momentary urge itself is experienced and worked out. Reference, that is, to larger organized wholes of meaning, overall goals, predispositions of value—as well as the "map" of the environment itself, with evaluation of resources and frustrations in terms of all these things. And if there were such a thing (as Goldstein pointed out, with reference to his frontal lobe cases), it would be very far indeed from anything we would recognize as healthy or effective human functioning.

To this model, as we have seen, Goodman adds the fundamental dimension of *awareness*. Contact, instead of being just a matter of chewing, is now equivalent to the awareness process itself (Perls et al., 1951, p. 275), since awareness is never given by the environment alone to the passive subject, but is itself an act of organization. Likewise, disturbance of contact is now seen not only or primarily as due to introjection of some foreign, "undigested"

8 7

authority, but as a problem in achievement of satisfaction, resulting from some disturbance in awareness itself (p. 290). Certainly, this is a richer and much more useful picture of functioning than was offered by the original Perls model. And yet Goodman, no doubt for some of the reasons examined in the previous chapter, still retains the episodic, impulse-in-isolation quality that marred and limited the earlier version. The crucial question of cumulative organization of experience, the *structured ground* in dynamic interaction with the emerging figure, still goes largely unaddressed.

Writers of the Cleveland School, working from the Goodman model, have proceeded to elaborate this analysis of *figure formation* into a diagnostic model in its own right, and, by implication at least, a new definition of healthy functioning (Polster & Polster, 1973, pp. 28 ff; Zinker, 1977, chap. 5). This model, known as the Experience Cycle, fleshes out the "life history" of a particular impulse or need (or gestalt formation) into stages roughly paralleling Perls's, which can then themselves be focused on in turn for the purposes of discriminative diagnosis and intervention. Schematically, the model is shown in Figure 1.

Exact terminology for the different stages varies slightly from author to author (Polster & Polster, 1973; E. Nevis, 1987; Zinker, 1977. Katzeff [1977] discriminates a seventh stage, "accomplissement," in the sense of consummation or satisfaction, in between "contact" and "withdrawal"); however, all the variations follow this general scheme. The same model with an ongoing time line (but still following the individual serial impulse in isolation) is shown in Figure 2. (Zinker, 1977, p. 97)

Either way, the consummation of the cycle is the moment or stage of *contact*, which is conceived here as the solution of the problem, and/or the actual engagement, physical or otherwise, with the desired goal or resource (which is to say, in either the Goodman or the Perls sense, which may not be the same thing, as will be taken up again below). Healthy functioning, again, is no more (and no less) than the smooth unfolding of this natural cyclic process—still without reference to how these cycles fit together, dynamically or hierarchically (Polster & Polster, 1973, pp. 39–45).

Following Goodman (Perls et al., 1951, p. 526), interruptions or disturbances to the cycle can then be classified in a typology of dysfunctions, symptoms, or "resistance" styles—all according to the particular *point* in the cycle at which the break or distor-

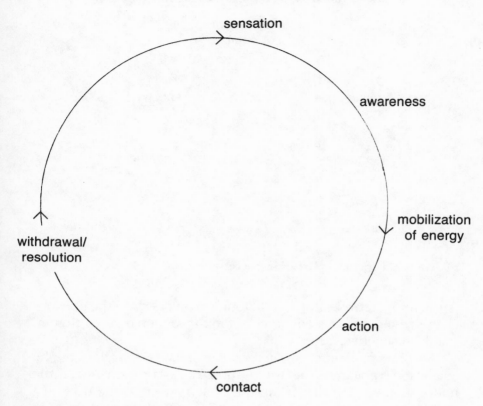

FIGURE 1. The Experience Cycle

tion characteristically takes place. Thus, a block in the sensation/awareness phase of the cycle (the difficulty in distinguishing these two as separate stages goes back to the unresolved question of whether a Perlsian or Lewinian notion of awareness is being used here) will produce dissociation, repression, possibly a conversion neurosis (i.e., classicial hysteria), or even psychosis (Zinker, 1977, p. 99). A block or departure from the cycle on the way from awareness to energy mobilization corresponds to introjection—or, in the Freudian model, to obsessive and self-punitive superego (and thus to depression, which both models see as following from an inhibition of aggressive energy, then turned against the self—retroflectively, as we would say here). Likewise, a break between energy and action could again be retroflection, in which the energy already mobilized by the need is diverted from its "natural" object and turned back against the self (confusion in the definition

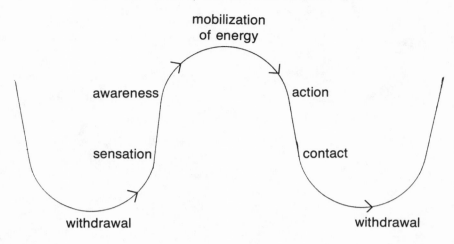

FIGURE 2. Experience Cycles in Succession

of the term "retroflection" itself, touched on briefly in the previous chapter, will be discussed more fully in the section on the Interpersonal Perspective, below).

At the same time, implicit in the model, regardless of the diagnostic typology of the interruptions to gestalt formation, is the notion that all disturbances in the cycle may be traced back to a problem in awareness itself—in the (somewhat limited) sense of full recognition and ownership of the immediate *need* that launched the cycle in the first place. This shows up clearly in treatment of the next characteristic breaking point of the cycle, between action and contact. If the person conceives a need or goal, has it clearly enough "in mind" to mobilize energy and then to take action, and still misses the mark, so to speak (that is, fails to achieve the thing desired in the first place), then almost by definition the action itself was misdirected or inadequately conceived or insufficiently powered from the start (leaving aside for the moment the possibility that the environment itself was just too resistant for the achievement of this particular goal). But this is tantamount to saying that the original problem was in the way the whole thing was conceived from the beginning. Characteristically, the person might have not quite dared, or allowed himself, to go after the thing he really wanted; or not have adequately surveyed the field for resources and obstacles; or have diminished the force of his own activity for any of a number of reasons, so that the resolution achieved is only partial; or have undergone any of a variety of other distortions or inhibitions to the way he was *conceiving* the problem, or the field, or himself—each with definite characteristic dampening effects on the robust, satisfying unfolding of the cycle, which is what healthy functioning in this view is all about (see Perls et al., 1951, pp. 288–96, for the flavor of this conception of the healthy ideal, which is very much tied up with the notion of living *passionately*).

This in turn points up an area of unclarity in the Experience Cycle model itself. Goodman, as we have seen, often used the terms "contact" and "awareness" synonymously, if not completely interchangeably. That is, awareness was itself regarded as a creative resolution or organization—"of the field," we would say, in Lewinian language—(Perls et al., 1951, p. 290). This is the problem-solving, or creative/artistic conception of the Gestalt perceptual model, which is certainly shared by Goodman and Lewin. Perls, on the other hand, with his much more Reichian approach, would have taken the initial impulse (the "awareness" in the cycle, the need state, but more physically conceived) much more for granted as a given, and focused on some actual physical contact along the lines of his own oral imagery. But which of these very different notions is intended here? If it is the latter, then are we not faced once again with a model which is best equipped to handle relatively trivial, primarily physical impulses, like thirst or exercise or going on a simple errand? But if it is the former, then how is the more elaborately conceived Goodman-type awareness achieved? Does it have a minicycle of its own, whose "contact" furnishes the "awareness" for this new cycle, and so on, in an infinitely regressive series? The point is not purely academic, because it bears on the question of how complex or how simple a case the Experience Cycle model is best equipped to handle. That is, as it stands, the Cycle seems to lend itself most naturally to application to Perlsiantype examples, which tend to be physical and simple (and indeed, this kind of example is the type most frequently found in the literature). But this in turn sacrifices the suggestion of Lewinian complexity—the organization of the field, awareness as an act of creative organization in its own right, leading to (or incorporating) the "creative adjustment," as the Goodman model seems to point toward. Thus, the tension between "Perls" and "Goodman" tendencies in the 1951 presentation is preserved in the Cleveland extension, along with the relative tendency to isolate figure from considerations of organization of ground.

The same type of difficulty arises with the introduction of the "sensation" stage at the beginning of each cycle. By starting with sensation, writers of the Cleveland group show a tilt toward the Perls/Reichian "body basis" for all awareness and action, which on other topics they move relatively away from (E. Polster, 1985; Melnick & S. Nevis, 1986). Goodman's general tenor is in the opposite direction. Thus, in the typical Goodman problem of a creative/aesthetic or cognitive/intellectual nature, I may well work on a solution (entirely in my head) until a sort of mental tension is relieved or dissolved, without ever having (or at any rate being aware of) any physical analogue to this tension at all. It is true that we speak, by analogy, of a problem "gnawing at" us, or "seizing" our attention, or the like (and even the term "concentration" itself is after all a physical image), but it does not follow from that that my attack and resolution and satisfaction in the "pure" problem-solving case are powered by *sensation* in anything like the same way as my satisfaction of thirst, or hunger—or even an angry or sexual urge. Thus, it is not clear quite how the Cycle model itself generalizes, from the simpler and physical to the more complex and cognitive cases, which are simply assumed to follow the same lines of development and resolution. Zinker, for example (1977, see especially chap. 5), asserts that the former are the building blocks of the latter, but does not show how this is the case.

Ironically, many of these difficulties with the Experience Cycle as an heuristic tool disappear when the case at hand is an organization or multiperson system instead of an individual person. This is because with a multiperson or nonsubjective system, the stages of formulation of a problem, on the one hand, and resolution or contact, on the other, are more readily and consistently distinguishable from each other than they are in a single person. Moreover, the issues of how to define the "contact" which results is less subject to Perls/Goodman crosscurrents at the organizational or systems level, where the goal state is generally some clearly external action or achievement. The irony of this is that the Experience Cycle model itself was generated for application to individual, subjective cases, and has been extended to the systems level only with some awkwardness of terms, particularly in the area of the "resistances" (Brown & Merry, 1987; Merry & Brown, 1986). The theoretical reasons for this awkwardness of fit, and a proposed revision aimed at solving the problem of application of the Gestalt diagnostic/prescriptive model at the systems level, will be taken up in Chapter V below.

THE GESTALT EXPERIMENT

Goodman, as we have seen, characterized therapy itself as a "safe emergency"—i.e., a place where the patient, in an overall setting of safety and trust, is nevertheless challenged to destructure familiar patterns of awareness and behavior and actually produce, not just talk about, a new organization of the self, under the exigency of having to deal with the "real" therapist in the "here and now" (Perls et al., 1951, pp. 293, 335). Thus, the characterization of Gestalt therapy as "phenomenological behaviorism" (Kepner & Brien, 1970)—phenomenological, in that it attempts to trace the structure of the client's own experience; and behavioral, in that it looks to a new behavior by the client, either within or outside the therapeutic session, flowing out of the new organization of awareness (a necessary and necessarily new "creative adjustment," to use Goodman's term). This is in direct and intentional contradistinction to the traditional Freudian model, which concentrates on the analysis of the "transference"—i.e., understanding the present behavior of the client (especially toward the therapist) with reference to its role in the organization of past, not present events. Here, by contrast, the therapist moves toward the "participant observer" role, in which present interaction is analyzed in terms of its own structure, with reference to the past as commentary on the present (Fagan, 1970; E. Polster, 1966, 1986). This is the reversal of the transference analysis discussed in the previous chapter. This too is the meaning of "present-centeredness," or concentration on the "here and now" in Gestalt therapy: not that past and future are not relevant, or are somehow inadmissible for discussion, but that they are used, again, as commentary or clarifying perspective on the *present* interaction or organization, which is under analysis in its own terms (E. Polster, 1985).

Out of this notion, of a reorganization of the field, and of behavior in the therapy hour itself, comes the idea of the structured Gestalt experiment. Zinker (1977), who has given the most elaborate and elegant treatment of the use of formal experiment in therapy, describes a process of some seven or more distinguishable steps in the mounting of one of these therapeutic mini-dramas, which are so much associated with the word *gestalt* in the popular mind: (1) groundwork—essentially a process of listening for a theme to work on; (2) contracting—a process in itself, of negotiating agreement with the client, that this topic will be pursued now, and in this particular way; (3) grading—this refers to calibration of the experimental task proposed, making it harder or easier (an elaboration of the contracting process, which Zinker credits to S. Nevis); (4) awareness/energy/support—(a compression of several of Zinker's stages) meaning the exploration of the client's "readiness stance," as he prepares to take the new step proposed; (5) enactment—the new action itself, which might be something directly interpersonal, such as telling the therapist of one's feelings about something he has done, or possibly something more psychodramatic, acting out a fantasy, speaking to an absent person or imagined part of the self, an internal voice, etc.; and (6) debriefing—the discussion of the new experience, how it felt, what it brings up, how it ties in with other experiences or feelings, past or present, and so forth (Zinker, 1977, chap. 6). This scheme, of course, roughly follows the stages of the Experience Cycle, and by virtue of that, would seem subject to the same criticism: namely, that the approach easily becomes "figure-bound," in the sense developed in previous chapters. It focuses on the "figure of contact" of the moment, obviously for the sake of having a "real" process to analyze and manipulate, and in clear hopes of coming to grips with a prototype or generalizable case of the client's "contact style"—but still at the cost of settling for a certain impulsiveness, an indifference to or relative avoidance of the question of stably organized features of ground, across situations and across time (features which would constitute a definition, in Gestalt terms, of personality or "character," another term, like "conscience," which is in particularly bad odor in Perls's view of things; Perls, 1947, 1973).

At the same time, the hallmark of a Zinker experiment is the enormous emphasis, as the stages outlined above would suggest, on the *interaction* between therapist and client (or, in a group setting, between client and other group members as well; 1977, chap. 7). In Perls's hands, this interaction in the experiment had been reduced to an absolute minimum (F. Perls, 1969a, 1969b, 1973). There the involvement of the client in choosing, shaping, grading the new behavior or task to be tried out was held basically to a simple yes or no: Perls instructed, and the client could take it or leave it (in which case Perls would move on to somebody more compliant—not without a therapeutic putdown in passing to the uncooperative subject). That is, with Perls, the activity in therapy tended to move away from experiment per se, as Zinker defines it (that is, as something constructed jointly and ad hoc, out of the immediate situation), and toward what Zinker calls an exercise (1977, chap. 6)—meaning something prestructured, that the therapist brings in. In the extreme, this could sometimes reach absurd lengths, as when Perls required an entire group to chant his "Gestalt credo," a familiar "poem" in which the speaker pledges fealty to a rigid and anomic autonomy,—or when he demanded that a client preface every statement with the phrase "here and now" (F. Perls, 1973; From, 1982).

In either case, though—interactive Zinker experiment or compliant Perlsian exercise—the question arises of whether, with all this elaborate structuring and instructing, the therapist is not in effect "reintroducing the couch," in Polster's felicitous phrase (E. Polster, 1985). That is, Freud's great discovery (which he came on by inadvertance, but brilliantly recognized for its potential) was that the key to change in psychotherapy, the dimension that brought the interpretive process to life, lay in the *present relationship* (however conceived) between therapist and client. It is true that by characterizing this relationship only in terms of "transference," he moved to throw the emotional meaning of the exchange back into the past, to downplay the present significance of present feelings (i.e., to retain the couch). Nevertheless, the door was opened, not only to effective therapy under his model, but also to further development and emphasis of the analysis of present interaction, present organization, as the focus of therapy. As discussed above, this emphasis is the very crux of the Gestalt approach, drawing, as we have seen, on Lewin's dictum that the *cause and meaning* of present behavior must be sought in present dynamics, with the past as reference, but not as unmediated cause (see Lewin, 1935, especially chaps. 3 & 4, for discussion of this unacknowledged contribution, without which the Gestalt model would be hard pressed to explain itself). At the same time, the focus on "here and now" interaction between client and therapist is the current trend of traditional, "neo-Freudian" therapy as well, in all but the most hidebound centers, deriving no doubt partly from the influence and competition of Gestalt and other "present-centered" therapies, but also partly from the concurrent development of object relations theory, which may give somewhat more direct causative weight to the past, but arrives at much the same point in terms of use of the present interaction in therapy (see for example Winnicott, 1986).

To turn around and rely extensively on therapist-directed experiments and exercises, which generally have an external, "third-party" focus (if not a purely intrapersonal one), is then to "reintroduce the couch" in this sense—i.e., to re-erect barriers or distance in the relationship between client and therapist, which is after all the most immediate, the most "real," the most authentically present "lab" both parties have, in the Goodman sense, for studying the crucial question of how the client organizes his subjective world, his interactions, his life. In other words, to build on Goodman's view of therapy as an experimental or safe emergency, it would seem that the actual and present "experiment," which is ongoing at all times in therapy, *is the behavior of coming to therapy* in the first place, the decision or stance, on the basis of only the sketchiest information and guarantees, to take up a new *attitude* toward one's life and problems, to treat them as exemplary material for study, not only as immediate problems in their own right, pressing for immediate solutions (with all the tension inherent in the deferral of that solution, in favor of that study)—and all of this in the intimate company of another person, a relative stranger, to whom one has ceded considerable authority, particularly in the area of one's own discomfort and dissonance in the face of painful or shameful material (since violation of expectation, destructuring of accustomed awareness structures, is what the process is all about).

But then viewed in this light, it would seem that the process of *contracting* for the experiment, which is so patiently and respectfully drawn out in the Zinker model, is considerably more interesting, and potentially more valuable for study and "experiment," than the official, formal "experiment" itself. That is, the whole business of how the client organizes and experiences mutuality, power, understanding or misunderstanding, self-revelation, hope and resignation, assertion and influence and affection and eroticism and work and play and so on, *in the contracting and negotiating process itself*, with another person under the particular conditions of therapy, is a richer field of study than how he performs or experiences the experiment, so-called, itself. But all this may well tend to get neglected as both parties turn their attention to the "task"—the "couch"—which has been interposed. Or rather, which has been introduced as a sample case, for both parties to use in studying the organizing patterns of one of them—but which then works to block or sidetrack that very study.

In the hands of a sensitive and instinctively mutual therapist like Zinker, no doubt these issues, these transactions, do get brought into the process for discussion, along the way and in the "debriefing" stage as well (1977). Unfortunately, as the literature shows all too clearly, not every Gestalt therapist is alive to the importance of these transactions themselves—to the process of therapy itself as an experiment, as food for study. As caricatures and self-caricatures of therapy (Freudian and otherwise) plainly show, it is easy to "do therapy," so long as one has a "couch" of one kind or another—a fixed structure and authority by which to control troubling interpersonal aspects of the process (and by which to know what to say next). Thus, "exercises" and even imaginative and tailor-made "experiments" easily become, in lesser hands, a substitute for dynamic theoretical understanding of the client, of people in general, and of productive (and safe) intervention for change. Thus the dictum attributed to Lewin, that "the most practical thing is a good theory" (Marrow, 1969),—because a good theory tells you what move to make when, and what not to make, and why. If the therapy itself is an experiment, why not track and negotiate and "debrief" *that*, as it goes along, without the introduction of other formal structures, whose very formality detracts from the interpersonal focus of the therapy? To go in the other direction, of heavy reliance on therapist-directed activities and implicit formal authority, is to remove the one best safeguard the client has against bad or destructive therapy (and to vitiate his best experiment at the same time): namely, his right and support to engage in mutual process, mutual feedback, to influence and resist and suggest and complain, as this intimate and delicate process unfolds—the very thing that was lacking, so often, in his own original, troubled experience of intimate dependency.

And finally, as mentioned above, we have to ask whether this serial activity, of setting up the "major experiment" of the hour—even in the aesthetic hands of a creative clinician like Zinker—doesn't reinforce the episodic, disconnected, impulse-of-the-moment tendencies already present in the Goodman model, and expressed again in the Experience Cycle, presented in isolation (as it easily is) from the context of stable and ongoing life structures. The result, in the common Gestalt phrase, may be "pieces of work" that remain just that:—pieces. "Meeting the client where he is," certainly a reasonable proposition and a welcome antidote to some of the Procrustean psychodynamic excesses, then becomes not "where he is" in any developmental process as theoretically understood by the therapist, or "where he is" in the unfolding of his own life and life issues, but rather just that: "where he is" at the moment, without direct regard for where he was last session, or last month—or where he is going, his goals, aspirations, values, commitments, and other structured features of his personal ground. The result may be "pieces of work" that repeat themselves, by the very fact of their fragmented nature: as Goldstein's work showed, the drive to make meaningful organizations of behavior at a higher level than the immediate "cycle" is inherent and an essential sign of health; when this drive is frustrated or not facilitated, the very Gestalt notion of a tendency to completion will mean repeated attempts to resolve the same thing (along the lines of Goodman's own explanation of the "repetition compulsion," so-called, discussed in the previous chapter).

"What shall we 'work' on today?" is a frequently reported question between Gestalt therapist and Gestalt client (Zinker, 1977). With overcontrolled clients, in overcontrolled times, the connections between these "pieces of work" may indeed have taken care of themselves by "organismic self-regulation." Today, it may often be the case that the "pieces" themselves—the isolated cycles from impulse formation to gratification—may not be the problem. The problem may rather lie in the missing connections between the "pieces" themselves—the formation of significant wholes of purpose, of commitment, of meaning—and of satisfaction and pleasure in a cumulative, not merely episodic, sense. In this case, it would seem that the Gestalt intervention of choice would be to dispense with formally structured "experiments," "exercises," and the like altogether, in favor of a sustained focus on the ongoing process of commitment to therapy per se, the "hanging in" (Perls's infantile "hanging-on bite," here rehabilitated; Perls, 1947, part II, chap. I)—and that the cumulative satisfactions, costs, losses, and new freedoms that accrue from sustained involvement, sustained passionate interest, may be the fruits of the one experiment the client has never undertaken.

THE INTERPERSONAL PERSPECTIVE

In the work of Perls, as we have seen, from 1947 through his posthumously published works in 1973, anything interpersonal is consistently devalued, by comparison with anything "autonomous." Other people, relationships, family, community, are all first relegated to the impersonal category of "environment," then left firmly behind in the "progress" from "environmental supports to self-supports," which Perls equates with the growth from infancy to maturity, or health (see any of Perls's works, especially 1973). Goodman's own deep ambivalence about the relation of social cohesion and individual development was discussed at length in Chapter III: in general, it can be said that while his theoretical formulation does not directly challenge Perls on this point (as does Lewin's work, for example), still he shows definite affinities for the other view. Among the "neurotic splits" Goodman hoped to address and heal with the Gestalt approach, for example, was the "false dichotomy" of "personal and social" dimensions (which is to say, exactly Perls's view), which leads, according to Goodman, to "formal and symbolic rather than real communal satisfactions," even among those "interpersonal therapists" (presumably Sullivanians) who would try to integrate these supposed poles, from some other theoretical base (Perls et al., 1951, p. 285).

Isadore From, also without directly challenging any of this on the theoretical level, nevertheless introduced and promulgated among his Cleveland students a significant refocusing of the model, back to a clearly positive evaluation of the interpersonal dimension. A good example of this shift of emphasis, without actually addressing the problem areas of the model itself, is From's approach to dreams. Where Perls would treat the dream purely as a projection, and direct the client to "play all the parts" (1969a, 1969b), in a sort of formally directed psychodrama or conversation, From takes a different tack. Drawing on the interpersonal potential of Perls's own "resistance" model, From takes the dream, by way of hypothesis at least, as a retroflection (From, 1978). That is, he tentatively regards the dream—particularly a dream occuring right before or right after a therapy session—as a case of the dreamer saying something *to himself*, that he inhibited himself from saying *to the therapist*. This creative reformulation, which is actually a new idea, going beyond both Perls's and Freud's (quite similar) dream approaches, then has the effect of shifting attention back to the therapist/client relationship itself, as the most powerful lab for study and experiment on the client's own process—exactly along the lines of argument in the critique given in the previous section.

So far has the Cleveland School gone in the direction of this From/Goodman emphasis, and away from Perls's solipsism, that in the end the processes of introspection, meditation, and solitude (not to mention masturbation, discussed in the previous chapter), tend to come out with a bad name. An example of this ambivalence about how to value these and similar experiences already mentioned above, is the Cleveland elaboration of the "resistance" of retroflection. With Perls, clearly, retroflection was the "turning back on the self" of the normal contact process—i.e., dental aggression —which is properly, unneurotically directed outward (indeed, as we have seen, to "chew" the environment is practically the only form of connection with it which Perls can admit as healthy; Perls, 1947, part II, chaps. III & XIII). But what to do, then, with the "self-supports"—taking care of oneself rather than looking to others to do it—which Perls equated with health itself, but which, under the Goodman model of *exchange* with the environment (including the social environment), may take on the appearance of a short-circuiting of a normal, healthy process? Which is the neurotic "resistance to contact:" the failure to cross the personal boundary aggressively, diverting that outward-bound energy toward the self instead; or the failure to *seek* a crossing of that boundary from the other person, lovingly, nourishingly, perhaps erotically (in Perlsian imagery, to "eat one self," so to speak—for example, by living in fantasy)? As a metaphorical case in point, how to evaluate masturbation—by definition an erotic experience with

the self, rather than with other people (as mentioned above, Goodman's attempt to classify this as a purely Perls-type retroflection
by ascribing an aggressive motive to the activity fails to clarify the
problem, for obvious reasons)?

The solution of the Cleveland model, here as in other cases
of an unresolved Goodman/Perls split, is to steer a double course.
This latter kind of self-directed activity, nourishing or pleasuring
the self, is also classed as a retroflection, but of a second, "Goodman" type. That is, in the first type, or retroflection-I, we have
the case of a failure to express one's own transactional urge
(whether aggressive, as in Perls, or affectionate, or otherwise), and
the consequent turning of it back onto the self. Self-punishment,
self-criticism, self-denigration are examples, but also taking care
of oneself, *if* that represents the directing-back (retroflection) of
an original caretaking impulse toward the other person. In the
second type, or retroflection-II, we have the reverse case. here the
desire to *be taken care of*—to be nourished, stimulated, talked to,
stroked, or otherwise sustained or pleasured—which *should be*
sought out and fulfilled for one by the other person, is instead done
by oneself, for oneself (see Polster & Polster, 1973, pp. 82 ff; also
Zinker, 1977, p. 103). In other words, we have now left Perls and
gone to the other extreme. Where with Perls, independence and
contact-as-oral-aggression were the ideal, and retroflection was one
of a number of possible failures (actually, possible consequences
of the original contact-failure of introjection), now the ideal is
contact-as-exchange, and any withdrawal into the self (as in the
Goodman view of introspection, mentioned above), is *also* a failure.
From a hypertrophied independence, we have arrived at the corresponding polar position, of mistrust or devaluing of any gesture
that does *not* cross the interpersonal boundary and involve the subject with another person. In the theoretical extreme, this would
be a move from compulsive isolation (Perls) to compulsive
gregariousness (Goodman; in practice, this extreme is considerably
softened in these same writers. See for example Polster & Polster,
1973; Zinker, 1977; L. Perls, 1982).

At the same time, and alongside this unclear theoretical area,
writers of the Cleveland group have been concerned with moving beyond the single-person focus of the Goodman/Perls model,
and of their own Cycle model as well. Zinker and S. Nevis, in particular, have extended the Cycle schema to an Interactive Cycle,

in which the motivational rhythms of two people are compared for analysis of points of juncture and disjuncture (Zinker and S. Nevis, 1981; E. Nevis, 1987). These same two writers have also explored the notion of shared or "middle ground," between members of a couple or other dyad. While their sense of the term "ground" is somewhat different from the notion developed in this critique, still this does take the "figure of contact" model in the direction of consideration of the *structure of background* as we have been advocating all through the argument here. If two people have certain shared areas to "fall back on" (the "middle ground" in their sense refers to areas of no- conflict between two people) in cases of conflict or divergence, then this does implicate the existence and analysis of enduring structures in the field that go beyond the question of the need or figure of the moment (see also Zinker & S. Nevis, 1985, 1986).

GROUP DYNAMICS

In the Perlsian group, not surprisingly, there is no "group dynamic"—or rather, there surely is one, but it is suppressed, and not regarded as relevant to the "work" going on (Perls, 1969b). Indeed, Perls was in the habit of scolding group members who attempted to offer any reaction or comments (or challenge) to his one-to-one work with a momentary "client" (1969b, 1973). Following From (and by implication, at least, Goodman), all this has been turned around in the work of the Cleveland School. Zinker (1977) exemplifies this shift of focus in his articulation of the "principles of Gestalt group process," which emphasize "group experience," "group awareness," "active contact between participants," and "the use of interactional experiments directed by the group leader" (p. 161). Clearly, this moves the "Gestalt group" (Cleveland version) away from the Perls model (and away from the traditional psycho-dynamic model as well, on which the Perlsian is constructed, with only the substitution of directed activity for directed interpretation), and toward something much closer to an "encounter" or process style of group therapy—only with the addition of structured experiments and exercises (see Yalom, Bond, Bloch, Zimmerman & Friedman, 1977).

There is no doubt that this is a useful and productive shift of focus, and yields a powerful approach to group work (Polster & Polster, 1973; Zinker, 1977). The only problem with this approach, in terms of the arguments developed here, is that it does not seem to follow readily from, or to be entirely reconcilable with, the terms of the Goodman/Perls model itself (the analysis of clear figure against "empty ground"), or of the Experience Cycle model, which is the creative elaboration of the original Goodman/Perls presentation. "Group experience" and "group awareness," in order to mean anything, must refer to the ongoing shared history of the group—i.e., what in group process terms are generally referred to as the norms, values, contracts, agreements (including agreed perceptions), purposes, roles, customary procedures, and so forth of the group. But these, in our terminology here, are structured features of the *ground* against which, or out of which, the particular transactions and issues of particular members are the "figures of contact" of the moment. As the Gestalt model itself (and Goodman in particular) should insist, it makes no sense at all to speak of, or try to make meaning of, a particular act or gesture in the group—say, an aggressive overture—without reference to relatively stable ongoing features of the kinds listed above. A hostile transaction has an entirely different meaning, obviously, at a Board meeting of General Motors, say, from the significance and sequellae it has in a therapy group (and a different meaning in a Cleveland Gestalt group from what it might have in a Perlsian Gestalt group, such as one might still find today among students of Perls; see for example Simkin & Yontef, 1984; also Zinker, 1977, p. 159). Same thing for a gesture of affection, or power, or support, or anything else. In all these cases, the *meaning of the figure* (of behavior—the gesture itself) will be given in the *structure of the ground*—i.e., the norms, goals, values, and so forth of the group.

Likewise, the focus on *interaction*, which Zinker advocates, does not seem to follow very clearly from the individually-centered, "figure-bound" model either. That is, if "clear figure" is the final and sole criterion of my own health, then what difference does it make to me, personally or theoretically, whether other agents in my "environment" have clear figure formation or not, if they are present to me, theoretically speaking, only as "resources?" It requires considerations of shared and ongoing history, of organized structuress of ground, *and the incorporation of these considerations into the theoretical definition of healthy functioning* along the lines proposed here, to make that link. The Cleveland group is quite right, and very much in tune with Gestalt psychological theory as presented here, to make these shifts of emphasis away from the Perlsian model, which was always more "early psychoanalytic" than "late Gestalt." But this important refocusing cannot be fully justified, theoretically, without recourse to the kind of thorough-going critique of the "figure-bound" model that we have been assembling here.

WORK WITH SYSTEMS

With the extension of the Gestalt model to work with families, organizations, and community systems, we enter an arena as foreign to Perls's thinking as it was to Freud's—and a region littered with the debris of failed attempts, from various theoretical perspectives, to generalize from the individual to the social/systems case (with the psychodynamic model accounting for perhaps the most debris; see for example Bion, 1958). To Goodman, by contrast, the idea of applying a psychotherapeutic model to a social- or community- or even world-level problem would not have seemed uncongenial (see for example 1947, 1960, 1962). Nonetheless, the attempt to make this leap, from the Goodman/Perls model, runs into the same difficulties as with the generalization to interactive or small-group cases: namely, the (by now) familiar problems that come with the concentration on figure when institutional forms (no matter how fluid or informal) are by definition organized structural features of *ground.*

One approach to the attempt to apply the given model to systems-level problems, without significant revision of the terms of the theory itself, is that of Brown and Merry (1987; see also Merry & Brown 1986), in their discussion of "neurotic styles" in organizations. Basically, this amounts to taking the familiar list of "resistances to contact" and drawing analogues at the organizational level to each of these "neurotic mechanisms" in turn. The result is a catalog or typology of theoretical dysfunctions, various ones of which may characterize various organizations or practices, either typically or at particular times and places. This perspective yields an interesting and useful new slant on diagnostic problems, but the limitations of it, by the argument here, would seem to lie in the normative flavor of the received model of the resistances themselves. That is, since not all "contact" can be equally nourishing or desirable for a given organization (or a given individual, for that matter), it is unclear exactly when a particular contact "choice" is a dysfunctional resistance, and when not.

An organization, generally speaking, has a particular purpose for existing, more or less clearly articulated in different cases, in a somewhat different sense from an individual—what is known in the organizational consulting field as a "core mission" (though in both kinds of cases the absence of felt purpose over time may be detrimental to health or even fatal). The given activities, chosen contacts, and even desirable or undesirable "resistances" of a given organization in a particular time and situation would seem to flow from the purposes and values of that organization—and not from a prior table of resistances or model of ideal contact. Thus it is not entirely clear exactly how to use the diagnoses of "organizational resistances" or "neurotic mechanisms," after they are generated. For example, a particular company may be run in a highly authoritarian manner, and even along aggressively competitive lines, vis-à-vis other companies—that is, with a high degree of introjection, internal confluence, projection, and probably retroflection as well (in the form of self-supports, and perhaps self-criticism). Indeed, the major sector of the Japanese economy is said to be run, and to all appearances fairly well run, along just such "neurotic" lines. But surely the evaluation of this style lies first of all in terms of the goals and productivity of that company, and not of some clinical ideal. Even looking at the case in "humanistic" terms, we may find that individual members are quite happy to live and work in this "neurotic" system, without necessarily being neurotic themselves—or at least that their degree of satisfaction is more related to their evaluation of the organizational hierachy and their own place in it, and to the organizational rewards system, than it is to their notions of how an "unneurotic" organization should look. Problems of this kind with the theory of the "resistances" in the 1951 model as a whole will be considered further in the following section of this chapter—and then taken up directly with the next chapter, where it will be argued that these same objections, offered here in the organizational case, apply to the original individual model of "resistances" as well, which calls for revision to bring out its full potential as a diagnostic and prescriptive tool.

A second approach to the Gestalt treatment of organizational problems is simply to apply the model, seriatim, to various significant individuals within the organization in question. This is at the heart of Herman and Korenich's work (1977), for example, and of much psychodynamic work with organizational problems as well. Certainly there is a place for this kind of individual counseling focus in systems work, depending on contractual factors and the like; but equally clearly it does not address many systems-level issues. Indeed, this approach sometimes seems to carry with it a denial that systems-level issues—organizational dynamics—exist at all, apart from individual personalities.

The most useful and imaginative extensions in the literature of the Gestalt model as applied to organizational or systems work are those of E. Nevis (1983, 1987). Nevis's thrust is to apply the Gestalt concepts of boundaries, part-and-whole relations, and the Experience Cycle model to the study of structures and processes of organizational life. The best way to study a system, in another dictum popularly ascribed to Lewin, is to try to change it—and then see what happens (quoted in Burke, 1980). As Nevis points out, under the Gestalt model the first change or intervention in the organizational field, from the consultant's point of view, is the entry of the consultant himself into the system (and note the parallel here with our view of the therapy contract and the therapy session themselves as the real experiment). The study of this contact between the established configuration and the new environmental figure (i.e., the consultant himself) then becomes a prototype for the study of other contact moments in organizational life, and of the organization's *style* of contact, particularly as expressed in its boundary configurations. Here at last we have a model of Gestalt application which, without directly addressing itself to some of the problem areas discussed in this analysis, still moves beyond these prior theoretical limitations to exploit the real potential of the Gestalt approach. From there, the consultant's work, broadly speaking, is concentrated in the awareness stage of the system's own "cycle"—thereby disequilibrating or destructuring the existing, possibly dysfunctional, "creative adjustments," at least potentially in favor of other, more comprehensive configurations that will represent a better resolution of the field in terms of the system's own goals. Thus while approaching the problem from quite a different entry point from that of this critique (the conditions and consequences of intervention, rather than the theoretical contradictions of the model), Nevis comes out at many of the same points as does the critical analysis of "resistance theory," particularly as applied to organizations, which is given in the following chapters.

THE ELABORATION OF THE
PERLSIAN MODEL OF THE RESISTANCES

In theory, as was discussed in Chapter II, the list of "resistances to contact" is endless. Perls referred, as we have seen, to at least twenty-two "avoidances" of contact (1947, p. 65) before settling on his list of four principal mechanisms for "not chewing": repression, introjection, retroflection, projection (p. 220). Volume I of *Gestalt Therapy* specifically adds desensitization (p. 191); while Goodman's Volume II list is projection, introjection, retroflection, confluence (again, his fear of the dead hand of social conformism), and egotism (p. 526—but in other places he lists many others (see pp. 511 ff). E. Polster (1973) adds deflection to the list, but omits Goodman's egotism (as does nearly every other writer in the field, as far as the present writer can determine; for a rare and thoughtful exception, see Latner, 1982). At least since 1973, then, E. Polster's list has stood as the standard canon, the "official" Gestalt catalog of ways to break, avoid, or diminish "contact."

But is breaking/avoiding/diminishing "contact" always and necessarily a bad thing? Is it not rather essential, to the individual and the larger system alike, to end some connections, avoid others, and attenuate or prefer still others—if only in the interests of managing time itself? The Cleveland School in general has been troubled by this unclarity in the Goodman/Perls model, which seemed to suggest that "contact" across the personal boundary was a preferred or ideal state, or that everything that was not a "contact" transaction should properly be at least a part of a cycle culminating in such a moment—and that everything else was neurosis. Part of the impulse for generating the Experience Cycle model in the first place, certainly, was to reintroduce the lost *time* element in the Goodman model—the need to lay groundwork and then build up to the full, satisfying contact moment—as well as to legitimize, in theoretical terms, a period of rest or withdrawal, punctuating the various "contacts" themselves.

In addition, the writings of the Cleveland School have tended to dwell upon the positive aspects of the various troubling "resistances," which by definition seem to be negative or inhibiting mechanisms in the flow of life. Thus, Zinker in particular (1977) stresses the artistic/creative aspect of projection, the positive ability to separate a part of the self from the self (the artistic product), or to make a leap of empathy into the world of another person, as one imagines it would be for oneself (pp. 8 ff). In the same way, positive sides of each of the "resistances" can be imagined: introjection—the capacity to cram for a test, for example, to memorize appropriately, or to "try on" some new idea; confluence—the ability to suppress difference and move cooperatively, as in dance, sex, or simply many practical aspects of group living; deflection—the ability to sidestep or defer some draining conflict or other encounter, to choose one's battles, to ignore provocation; and retroflection—as discussed above, the capacity to take care of oneself, something about which the Goodman model, and the Cleveland elaborations, show some ambivalence. In all these ways, the old, "bad" resistances suddenly seem to take on a new shine, as positive coping strategies, in some situations, or even as clear creative capacities, without which the person would be handicapped in various areas of life (imagine an employee who could never introject, a lover without some element of confluence, even a prizefighter, say, who could never deflect blows but had to meet them all head-on, "man-to-man," as Goodman puts it [Perls et al., 1951, p. 293]).

The trouble is, of course, that now that we have rounded out the picture of "resistances," they no longer seem so much like "avoidances of contact" in the negative sense at all. Or at the very least, we have lost our clear "autonomous criterion" for when we are dealing with a "good resistance," and when with a "bad." As Goodman said of the multiplying entities of Freudian mental geography, in place of one unclear concept we now have two unclear concepts (Perls et al., 1951, p. 301). For how are we to know, in the terms of the model, when a given introject, say, is a creative or necessary coping strategy and when it is a deadening, life-inhibiting "resistance to contact"? At least in Perls's model, we knew (instances of introjection were all bad, except perhaps in the case of group members introjecting Perls's directions). And if we cannot know, then how are the "resistances" to be used to analyze, much less to diagnose/evaluate, individual or systems cases? It is to these difficult but potentially clarifying questions that we will turn our attention in the next chapter.

C H A P T E R **V**

The Resistances Reconsidered

THE ORGANISM lives, in another one of Goodman's brilliantly simple formulations, by maintaining its difference from the environment (Perls et al., 1951). We might add, very much in the Goodman spirit (if not the Perlsian), it lives by maintaining its difference *and* by relaxing that difference at the boundary, so as to find/assimilate some part of the "unlike" environment which is "like" enough, or can be made "like" enough, to serve as nourishment (and thereby changing itself in the process). Food, according to Aristotle (as quoted by Goodman, p. 270), is that which is unlike, or novel, which can become like, or harmonious—that is, it loses its difference. Thus the two poles of the organism's continued survival and growth: resistance, and accommodation—or, in Gestalt terms, confluence. Both poles are essential to life—which is to say, to *contact*, in the sense of a structured encounter between organism and environment ("at the boundary," as Goodman would say). This is true whether the "organism" in question is an individual person or an organized system of persons—an "organization," a couple,

1 1 0

a family, a group, a society. The same principles have to apply: if not, we would not be able to speak of the identity of the "organism" at all. Without *organization*, which is to say, without *boundary* (of figure against ground, the "me" against the "not me"), it would not exist at all as a separate entity—and we would not be able to see it. Without "resistance" in this sense, the entity would simply merge into the field. At the same time, without some element of confluence at the boundary, some relaxation of this resistance, the same system or entity would soon perish—and then "de-compose," which means to become one with the field again.

Thus it is meaningless to speak of contact without any reference to resistance *and* confluence, which are the two poles of contact itself, the inherent dynamic tension of "otherness," or existence itself—of which the ongoing resolution is the "creative adjustment" Goodman speaks of. There can be no system, or organism, which is "out of contact" in this sense—for more than a moment or two at a time—with the environment. The very definition of the "organism" is the *boundary in the field*. And that boundary, as Goodman says (Perls et al., 1951, pp. 269–70), both separates *and* joins the organism/environmental field. That is, it is not so much the point or arena of contact as it *is* the contact—in whatever form, whatever type or style of encounter, it takes in the moment. Without ongoing exchange, the "organism" quickly ceases to exist. For exchange to take place—any exchange, breathing, eating, learning, manipulating, even visual perception—resistance must be relaxed—but not too far, or disintegration will be the result. By the same token, similarity, or confluence, must be allowed or created—but not too much, for the same reason. These processes or functions *are* the processes and functions of contact, of structured encounter/relation with the environment, of exchange. To say that "contact" is one thing but "resistance to contact" is another—and then to add that "confluence" is a special case of this resistance (specifically, the resistance of insufficient resistance)—is to confuse terms hopelessly. The fundamental premises of the Gestalt approach—the universality of the figure/ground relationship, of boundaries, of the organism/environment field—do not allow it. And Goodman's own discomfort with the "resistance" language of his own model is manifest (see Perls et al., 1951, v. II, chap. XV, for example): it contradicts the whole thrust of the model he constructs so eloquently in Part I of the same volume.

Of course, the organism can be "out of contact" with, or oblivious/desensitized to, certain *parts* of the environment (or, by extension, with parts or subsystems of itself). By the same token, features of the environment (or the self) can be "out of awareness"—and, as Goodman (sometimes) says, contact is awareness, a structured perception/encounter with the environment (or awareness plus aware behavior (Perls et al., 1951, p. 270). Neurosis (again in Goodman's phrase) is "creative adjustment" (i.e., contact) "of a field in which there are repressions" (p. 522). But when we say "repressions," clearly we mean something more than just "out of contact" or "out of touch" things: we mean awareness, or potential awareness, which is dynamically *held* out of "contact," out of the usable field. If they were simply far away, or forgotten, or unknown to the subject, or momentarily ignored, then we might speak of ignorance, or an "inadequate data base," but hardly of repression. But then to "hold" something dynamically *is*, again, a kind of contact—specifically, a split-off or rigidly bounded kind (and a feature, at the same time, of the structured *ground* of subsequent or concommitant contacts).

And how is this feature, this "repressed" material, "held out of awareness"? Basically, it must be either by a too-rigid *resistance* (an impermeable boundary, not allowing any "point of contact") or by a too-thoroughgoing *confluence* (that is, a blurring of the distinction between this feature and the self, or this feature and the rest of the environment, so that you cannot "see" it). Or, turning this around, the repressed material is held out of awareness either by *too little resistance* at the boundary (i.e., merging) or by *too little confluence* (i.e., rigid exclusion, or hypertrophied resistance). Either way, we see again that the dynamic polar process of resistance/confluence at the boundary is not something subversive of or opposed to "contact"—but *is* the contact process itself. And that the particular "mix" or rhythm of these poles is the particular style or flavor of that transaction, that awareness pattern, that contact. And, finally, that distortion or dysfunction in that process (in this case, repression, which is a particular case of frozen or unusable contact) is not due to the *introduction* of "resistance" (much less of "*a* resistance," such as "confluence") into an otherwise pure and uncontaminated contact process, but is rather a matter of the underdevelopment of one functional pole of the contact dynamic and the corresponding overdevelopment of the other.

By definition of "boundary," of organism-in-the-field, some mix of both is always necessary for any "contact" at all to take form and be registered.

To repeat, what we are saying here is that there is no such thing as "contact" in some ideal, platonic form, pure and theoretical, which then in the "real" case becomes unfortunately sullied with "resistances"—confluence, projection, introjection, deflection, and all the rest. Rather, the exercise of all these modes, all these variables at the boundary, which we will call "contact functions," *is* the contact, which can then be described, analyzed, and possibly even categorized by its particular mix of such modes or functions— but does not exist at all without them. Take away all resistance, and all confluence, and all the other "resistances" (as will be argued below), and what is left is not "contact" at all, pure or otherwise, but only a complete merging, or possibly a dead body, pending decomposition, which is finally, completely, and for the first time "out of contact."

Now obviously, this contradicts or reorganizes most what has been said about the "resistances" in the literature so far under the Gestalt model. And yet, as was argued at the outset of this chapter, this view is the natural and logical consequence of that model, when stripped of its various (mostly psychodynamic) accretions and taken to its own creative/logical conclusion. The "resistances" (as was discussed in chapter II) were a direct incorporation, or introjection, on Perls's part, from psychodynamic theory. The only change in the transition was that where in the earlier Freudian model the "defenses" were first of all defenses against the psychotherapist, in Perls's formulation this was opened out to "resistances to contact" in general (Perls, 1947, p. 65). And even this followed closely along the lines laid down by Anna Freud in 1937, in her definitive codification of the "mechanisms of defense" for psychoanalytic theory (nor would Anna Freud have had any difficulty with Perls's modification of her model, as long as the "contact" resisted was understood to be contact with repressed libidinal/aggressive material from the Id. And since, as we have seen, to Perls "resistance to contact" was by definition resistance to one's own oral/destructive impulses, even this slight distinction between them would tend to disappear).

Goodman (with some discomfort, as noted above) then took over the Perlsian resistance model in turn—also, we might argue, by a process of introjection, or "failure to chew thoroughly," since the terms of the Perlsian/Freudian resistance model, to resume the argument above, are not really reconcilable with the fundamental modifications Goodman had already made, in Volume II of their collaboration, to Perls's own "transitional" version of the Gestalt approach (see Perls, 1947, 1969a). But by shifting the emphasis in the definition of contact from chewing to awareness, or at least "aware behavior," Goodman correspondingly shifts the meaning (by implication, at least) of resistance somewhat—from "resistance to contact" to "resistance to awareness." But then this latter formulation, if only he would adhere to it more thoroughly, would then be much more congruent with the basic terms of his own model—since the troublesome notion of being "in" or "out of" contact could then be replaced by consideration of the organization and style of particular contact moments, and of the ground, in which they occur. All the resistances would then become, ultimately, variations on *repression* (just as they are in the Freudian model)—in place of *introjection*, which is the key resistance to Perls, from which all others flow. However, repression itself, as argued above, has to be regarded as a particular case of dynamic contact; and then the rest of the model, the catalog of "resistance types," cannot stand as *opposed* to contact, in the way that Goodman has outlined them, but rather must be regarded too as "types" or "modes" of contact itself.

But then what of these other "resistances"—besides confluence and "resistance" itself, which we have maintained are the basic conditions or dimensions of contact, and not in and of themselves "avoidances" of it? What, specifically, of projection, introjection, retroflection, egotism (Goodman), and deflection (Polster)? The same argument that was made for confluence and for "resistance" itself can be made again here. That is, if it is completely impossible to conceive of "contact" that does not operate, in part at least, by modulation of the functional modes of resistance and confluence, it is nearly as difficult to imagine a contact process, a transactional/organizational act "at a boundary," which does not modulate along the lines of these other "functional modes" as well, which up to now we have known as "resistances."

Take introjection, for example—the "taking in" of material without destructuring it, breaking it down, and thus by implication uncritically, as we have been saying Perls and Goodman took in the psychodynamic "defenses," never really making them the new model's own. Not only are there positive, functional, even necessary aspects to introjection (in learning, for example), as mentioned in the previous chapter on the Cleveland School; more than this, it is difficult to describe any process of incorporation that does not contain an element or stage, at least, of introjection. Certain spiders and insects, it is true, have the capacity to spray or inject their food with a "tenderizer," so that it is predigested before eating; but short of this, generally speaking, "taking in" has to precede "destructuring," to some degree at least. A rigid refusal to do this would make the learning of any new idea or skill much more difficult, if not impossible. Certainly, it is easy to see where too much introjection could become dysfunctional, a distortion of the contact process (or better, a contact process of a particular, distorted kind), in terms of the goals of the organism; but the same is true for too little, which would be the obsessive chewing of everything, as in compulsive argumentation, even fear of choking or possession by dybbuks. What is not so easy is to imagine any contact, any organization/transaction "at the boundary," which did not include some element, provisional or long-term, of introjection. In other words, here again we seem to be dealing not so much with a *resistance* to contact, in the sense of a refusal or break, as with yet another *function or mode* of contact, another dimension or channel of the contact process. Another approach, so to speak, to organizing the encounter, which may be more or less useful according to the goals of the person or system at the time, and the "truth of the situation" (to repeat Goodman's phrase about appropriateness in therapy). Take away the "introjection" (and the "resistance," and the "confluence"), and what you have is not pure contact, or ideal contact—but no contact at all.

The same line of argument can then be applied to the other "resistances" of the established list: retroflection, projection, Goodman's egotism, Polster's deflection. How can there be any "contact," any organized meeting or resolution of the field at all, without some element of self-support, and possibly suppression of some outward-directed gesture in favor of another (retroflection); some putting out of something, or imagining where another person is, so as to find him for the encounter (projection); some conservation of ego/self boundaries, even in the moment of contact union (egotism); some deferring or inhibiting or dulling of some things, some possible contacts, in favor of others chosen for concentration at the moment (deflection)? Here we see how right the Cleveland School has been to emphasize the healthy, positive aspects of the various "resistances" (Zinker, 1977; Polster & Polster, 1973). All that we would add here, to their shift of emphasis, is that they did not push the revision far enough. Far from being "resistances to the contact process which nevertheless have a potentially positive side, sometimes, in moderation, under unspecified conditions"—all these terms, taken together, *are* the contact, are the "ways of meeting at the boundary." To repeat, there is no other "contact" apart from or not made up of these various modes or functions. It makes no sense to speak of "introjection," say, as by definition a "resistance to contact," any more than it does to speak of its opposite polar function—"chewing," to use Perls's own polarity—as necessarily or by definition a "resistance to contact." Either one may be used to "resist" (in the somewhat different sense of distort or attenuate) the particular "figure of contact" of the moment, or to enhance and heighten it, depending on the goals and style of the particular organism/environmental field in question at a particular moment. But it is difficult to imagine the "contact" that did not include, again, some element of both.

Rather, we would say here that contact which was characterized (especially habitually characterized) by a heavy reliance on the introjection *function* (or the chewing function, for that matter) would be contact of a particular kind, well suited to certain goals and processes and ill-suited to others. But all contact is necessarily characterized by the use and blend of some particular contact *functions* in this sense of the term, and not others (or at any rate, not to the same degree). Practically anything, any act or flavor of exchange, may be a "resistance"/distortion of the contact process—or a facilitation of that same process, all depending on the relation of those modes or functions to the *goals* of the organized encounter in question. But then it is to those goals, those organizations, that we must look for evaluation of the "contact" itself—and not to a certain arbitrary list of single halves, of inherently bipolar functions (bipolar, because any function, any mode, has an extreme, and that extreme has an opposite extreme; also because of the inherently bipolar nature of the "problem" of contact in the first place, which is simply that of the organized entity which is bounded from *and* bound to the environment, and which must always live in the tension of that bipolar condition).

It is ironic that Goodman, in his quest for "autonomous criteria" of functioning, stopped short of seeing how this adaptation of the Freud/Perls model (this introjection, as we have been calling it) opened the door again to the very kind of clinical labeling, the reified "character types" and the extrinsic standards of human personality, that he hoped to avoid (see Perls et al., 1951, pp. 523 ff; and for an example of old-style "clinical name-calling," under the Perls/Goodman terminology, see for instance Crocker, 1981). This quest, this hope,—which amounts to the question of whether an ethics, a system of values, can be derived from the terms of human nature itself—is something, we would argue, that still may be answered in the affirmative. But the answer, if it does come, will lie in revising the "figure-bound" Goodman/Perls model to accommodate the "real-life" contextual processes which lie *behind* figure formation in the moment (and which consist of the selection of certain contact *functions*—not "resistances"—over others, according to dispositions of style, situation, goal, *and values*).

That is, if the nature of the organism can be defined, then that may lead to the ability to evaluate certain contact functions over others, for certain purposes or goals—in other words, to a behavioral ethics based on psychological description. But such an ethics, and such clinical criteria, cannot be derived from arbitrary normative lists of "neurotic resistances" without reference to those processes, those contact goals themselves.

Here then we can see the theoretical link between our critique of the model of the resistances, as traditionally conceived, and the proposed revisions to the "figure-bound" model of gestalt formation developed in Chapters I through III. Take for example the case of deflection. In the discussion above, we were making the argument that for any contact, any given organization to be achieved, other potentially competing needs, urgencies, figures, or ways of organizing the field must be deflected, somehow or other, at least temporarily. Other "contacts" that present or threaten must somehow be deferred, damped down, selectively unattended to, "bounded off," deenergized, repressed, and so forth, so that this particular contact, this need or organization favored over the others, can come to the fore (and unfold along the lines of the Cleveland Experience Cycle model). If I wish to have a marriage, for example, I may have to deflect or otherwise manage my urges for certain other relational experiences—and by no means only sexual ones. By the same token, if I want to have a sexual experience, I have to inhibit/deflect other, distracting figures of concern or interest. If I pursue one career, I do not pursue all the others, and so on. All this may happen "naturally," without my being much aware of it, or it may require great thought and hard choices. But it certainly happens, one way or the other. No contact at all can be achieved, no organization can be realized, without this crucial function of deflection, of all the rest of the infinitude of possible contacts and organizational choices in the moment.

But this focusing/defocusing, this *selection* of one figure over other, competing exigencies and interests, amounts to saying that there are after all crucially relevant processes going on *outside figure formation itself* (and in support of it, or no figure could be formed). Without this consideration, the notion of figure/ground itself becomes meaningless. But these processes, by definition, *are features and activities of ground*—which, as we see, comes to seem by this analysis a more and more busy and structured place, and not at all the "empty" domain characterized as healthy by Goodman (Perls et al., 1951, p. 299). If certain selections, certain preferences, are *habitually* valued by the subject over certain others (as must of course be the case, or life would indeed be the serial dream of the somewhat lobotomized isolate who emerges from a literal reading of the Goodman/Perls model), then these choices, those selections, are *structural features* of the personal ground, which must be considered in any "gestalt analysis," as much as or more than "figure formation" itself—if only because these *structures of ground* are the *conditions* of figure formation, the prerequisites and determining factors in the particular *kind* of figure achieved, in various situations. Once again, it is the insistence on taking *figure in isolation* from ground as the relevant study that introduces all these problems and distortions into the theory—including both the episodic nature of the Perlsian model in particular and the possibility of a notion of "resistances to contact" at all, in the traditional Goodman/Perls sense.

Let us now restate the argument thus far in schematic form. Under the Perls/Goodman model of contact and resistances, the picture looks like this:

CONTACT	VS.	"RESISTANCES"
		— introjection*
		— projection
		— retroflection
		— confluence
		— egotism (Goodman)
		— deflection (Polster)

(*In the original Perls model, introjection itself would be a heading, with the others as subsidiary variations.)

whereas, in the revision proposed here, the scheme would look like this:

CONTACT
(vs. isolation, anomie, nonexistence or complete merging)

resistance/differentiation	vs.	confluence
projection	vs.	retention, literalness
introjection	vs.	chewing, destructuring
retroflection	vs.	exchange, encounter
egotism	vs.	merging, yielding
deflection	vs.	focusing, concentration

In the revised table, as we have seen, the so-called "resistances" are redefined as *dimensions or functions of the contact process*, which in turn is redefined comprehensively here as the *organization of the subject in the field* (a definition which takes in both the Perlsian emphasis on exchange and the Goodman formulation of "creative adjustment," with or without full awareness). *Each* of the "contact functions" or modes (as well as many others) may then function as a facilitation or an inhibition of the "good contact" process, depending on the development (or over- to underdevelopment) of that particular mode, the development of its polar complement, the flexibility of movement between poles and among functions—and the particular goals which organize the system in general and the given contact in question, in particular.

Once again, as we have seen with Perls, Goodman, and Anna Freud as well, there is nothing sacrosanct about any particular list of "resistances," traditionally conceived—or "functions," as we are redefining them here. The number and nature of the contact functions that are relevant for consideration in a given case will be derived not from some standard list (although, "organismic" needs being finite, a standard list is a perfectly reasonable place to start), but from considerations of the particular functions a given organism/organization needs to achieve its particular goals in a given field. In practice, the significant functions of organizations may be thought to vary more than those of individuals, or even of families, because of the more widely varying life purposes, or "core missions," of organized multiperson systems. However, even with individual or family systems, it is important to remember the great variety in contact processes (or "defensive styles," to use the older psychoanalytic language, from which the Perls/Goodman terminology directly derives) among individuals or families in different societies, different social classes or milieus—or simply different stages of life. Thus, in our society at any rate, it is considered appropriate and even essential for healthy development for an infant to exhibit a high degree of confluence in contact in the first year or so of life (a good nurser, a good "bonder," with a high degree of body-conformity or "molding" when held), but a correspondingly (and oppositely) high degree of *differentiation/resistance in contact* (not resistance "to" contact, as any parent of a two-year-old knows) in the second and third years. In the same way (and at the other end of the life cycle), both Jung (1939) and Erikson (1951) propose that the mode or degree of *egotism*, of *assertion of the bounded self*, which is appropriate and functional earlier in life, becomes less so in old age, where the central task or goal of the individual becomes one of finding harmony or meaning in an extrapersonal context. Once again, the "contact dimensions" or "contact functions" which are appropriate and important for analysis, diagnosis, and intervention are determined by consideration of the particular goals and values (i.e., by particular institutionalized preferences and tendencies in the personal ground) of the "organism" in question at the time—and, for that matter, consideration of the goals and values of the intervener, the change agent him/herself.

Even under the rather authoritarian psychodynamic system, we saw a certain flexibility of the conception of "defenses," according to cases. Thus, Anna Freud (1937) codifies the "official canon" of nine defenses—regression, repression, reaction formation, isolation, undoing, projection, introjection, "turning against the self" (presumably something like masochism), and reversal (p. 43)—but then goes on to add, at various points in the text, sublimation, fixation, somatization (conversion), phobia itself, identification with the aggressor, "altruistic surrender" (clearly a self-diagnosis, on her part), contemptuous disparagement, transformation of affect, displacement, condensation, omission, "Charakterpanzerung" (Reich's body armor, which fascinated Perls), suppression of affect, denial (which seems to be a rather overarching term, taking in all the rest as special cases), and obsession itself (elsewhere generally regarded as a neurotic *type* with its own characteristic array of defense mechanisms). Clearly, the sheer volume and variety of the catalog, taken together with Anna Freud's own recognition of the essential role of "defense mechanisms" in healthy living (pp. 173 ff), begin to point toward a revision of the whole concept of "defense" or "resistance," along the lines of the argument taken up here: namely, a reexamination of all these "mechanisms of avoidance" as *ways of encountering the world* , as components of organized functioning, well *or* ill, and not purely as blocks in that same functioning (or diversions of some primal energy or drive, as in Freud and Perls). However, Anna Freud is of course inhibited from taking the implications of her own reformulation any further by the terms of libido theory itself, under which the central problem of the "organism" is defined not as the organization of self-in-environment, but the precarious management of potentially overwhelming internal drives.

Perls too, for his part, while reframing aggression as a basically healthy function and giving lip service to the importance of the organism/environment relationship, still retains the psychodynamic notion of "resistances" as ways of refusing or avoiding that relationship, rather than as expressions or structures of that connection, that organization itself. And like Anna Freud, he is then left with the conceptual untidiness, at the least, of the way these "avoidances" seem to spin themselves out without any theoretical limit, potentially becoming equivalent to all the possible functions or activities imaginable for an organism (perhaps with the single exception, for Perls, of chewing). And like the Freuds, he is also unable to say, from a theoretical point of view, when any one of these functions reaches the point of neurosis, and when it is a healthy compensation, or compromise at least. But these theoretical awkwardnesses would seem to suggest that there is something wrong with the basic conception, as we have been arguing here. In addition, while both Perls and Anna Freud may choose to draw up a particular list of these conceptually troublesome functions, neither of them can give any reason for stopping there, and not continuing ad infinitum.

In the lefthand column in the chart below, by way of illustration, is a *partial* listing of the various activities or modes of action mentioned by Perls in 1947 as "avoidances" or "resistances."

scotoma (blind spot)	clear vision? focusing?
selectivity	randomness? impulsivity?
inhibition	"exhibition"
repression	expression
flight	approach
overcompensation	yielding? undercompensation?
armor	permeability
obsessions	free associations?
permanent projection	literal-mindedness?
hallucinations	realism
complaints	acceptance
intellectualism	emotionalism? action?
mal-coordination	grace
displacement	facing things?
sublimation	passion? factuality?
"many character features"	fluidity
symptoms	stoicism?
feelings of guilt and anxiety	indifference? psychopathy?
projections	ownership?
fixation	lability
indecisiveness	commitment, fixation
retroflection	expression, dependency
annihilation	acceptance, nurturing
hypertrophic growths	hypotrophic growths
changes and distortions	steadiness, factuality
introjection	chewing
confluence	differentiation, resistance

The righthand column, obviously, lists possible poles or opposite functions to Perls's terms of "resistance." We say "possible poles," because clearly these terms themselves might have a considerable variety of "opposites" depending on how they are conceived in a given context. Once again, the argument here is that in each case *either* term, either pole (or other poles), may be the "resistance," while all of them, under various circumstances and for various purposes, may be essential to the very "contact" Perls would see them as blocking. In some cases (selectivity, for instance, or confluence/differentiation, as discussed above), it is impossible to imagine any contact at all, any organized encounter or exchange, which did not include some use of that function. Any and all of these terms may be seen equally as resistances to contact, channels of contact, styles of contact, facilitators of contact, distortions or blocks in contact, and so forth—again, depending on the hyper/hypotrophy of the functions themselves, the flexibility of range along that bipolar continuum in each case, and the *goals* of the "contact" in question, under the particular field conditions given.

But what does this new view of the "resistances" and of contact, and of the functional relations between them, mean for diagnosis and intervention, at individual and systems levels? First of all, the strengths of the traditional Gestalt approach are enhanced, not sacrificed, by this change of perspective on "resistance." Even in psychoanalytic work, since Anna Freud's time it has been customary to speak of "analysis of the defenses," along with "analysis of the transference" or of the "instinctual vicissitudes," as the essence of therapy. In terms of the argument here, this was already, in and of itself, a step in the right direction—a step toward a "process" therapy such as Gestalt or possibly object relations work, along the lines we have developed here. That is, to speak of a patient's "defenses," or "defensive style," is at least to try to talk about how he organizes the present encounter, how he structures his own self/environmental field, for exchange and meaning, in present time and by present dynamics.

Likewise, when Zinker (1977) and the Polsters (1973) speak of "working with the resistance," or "going with the resistance," what they are doing, in our terminology here, is exploring the *contact style* of the patient—and not necessarily the things the patient does "instead of contact," as the previous model would imply. (Indeed, by our argument there are no such things; the subject is always "in contact" of some kind. The question, always, is what kind, and is it appropriate to the goals of the patient, and the conditions in the field?) In other words, if there is validity and practicality to the theoretical revisions developed here—specifically, the consideration of *structured ground* and the related shift from "resistances" to "contact functions" (of which the preferred and habitual modes are examples of structures in the ground)—then it should not be surprising to find that experienced and gifted practitioners are already working in this way. On the contrary, if the model developed here is as "lifelike" and as congruent with basic terms and concepts of Gestalt theory as we have argued it is, then it would be very surprising indeed if successful practitioners, therapists and consultants, were *not* already in some practical harmony with these considerations. The question is whether the theoretical base of this work supports the most effective, most successful work under this model—or whether that "best work" does not have to be done, in some areas, "against" or in spite of some terms of the existing theory itself. The contention here is that the best work done under the Gestalt model, both with regard to the "resistances" and with regard to the figure/ground process, is more congruent with, and better explained by, this revised model than it is with and by the original Perls/Goodman presentation in these areas (see for example E. Polster, 1985, for some related concerns, expressed by a master Gestalt therapist).

At the same time, certain contradictions or murky areas of the received model are clarified by these revisions. An example is the functional contact process of "retroflection," discussed in the previous chapter. The traditional model seemed to glorify an idealized "contact," while (therefore) disparaging the "resistances" that were seen as getting in the way of that full, ideal state. The problem then was how to regard and classify activities in general in which the person did not cross or engage at the "contact boundary" with the environment, but remained within the bounds of his own personal system. In some of these cases, to be sure, the "failure" of "contact at the boundary" was due to an inhibition of *expression*, a fear or inability to express aggression, desire (sexual or otherwise), power, and so forth. These are basically the kinds of truncated gestures Perls had in mind when he coined the term. But what about the other kind of "staying within the personal boundary," in which the person "fails" to *seek* something from the environment (nourishment, stimulation, clarification, information, and so forth), and instead provides the resource from within himself? Now in Perls, this very "neurosis" or "resistance" ("retroflection-II," as we called it in the previous chapter) was virtually the definition of health, which was equated, as we have seen, with an extreme self-sufficiency (stemming, no doubt, more from issues in Perls's own personal history than from any implications of the Gestalt psychology model). With Goodman, to repeat, this view of retroflection is basically preserved, only with some ambivalence about the absolute health of the isolated Perlsian autonomous man, whose connection with the environment seems to modulate only from expressive force to aggressive intake (Perls et al., 1951, pp. 532 ff). At times Goodman lets this formulation stand; then again, at other times he seems almost to reverse it, as we have seen above (again, see for example Perls et al., 1951, p. 532).

Then with the Cleveland School and the important influence of From, this ambivalence (or hesitation about the Perls doctrine on health) increases, to the point where choiceful solitude, introspection, reflection, or meditation seem to become slightly suspect, as was discussed in chapter IV (and see Perls et al., 1951, p. 178: "In the long run, any interpersonal contact is better than retroflection"—but Perls's own definition of health *is* retroflection!). This extreme is countered by the thoughtful voice of Cynthia Harris, of the Cleveland Institute (quoted in Zinker, 1977, p. 103), who points out that "retroflection is the mark of a civilized society" because it permits social order, in place of raging individual impulsiveness. This view in turn is close to that of Freud,—the pessimistic Freud of *Civilization and its Discontents* (1930)—that is, that the price of civilization is the sacrifice of the "basic instinctual nature" of man, or, at best, its delayed, deferred, or sublimated gratification. However, under the revised Gestalt model we have been citing and developing here, the "basic instinctual nature of man"—if it is useful to employ such a phrase at all—is not the isolated libidinal or aggressive urge, but *organization itself*, the capacity and necessity for forming meaningful wholes, at ever higher, ever more inclusive levels (once again, see Goldstein, 1939, 1940). To defer or subsume one gestalt, one need, one contact, in favor of another which is of a higher order of urgency is not a block or a break in "good contact" or healthy process, but is the very essence of that organized contact process itself. To argue otherwise is to oversimplify the Gestalt model into a kind of equal series of urges in succession, just as we have been arguing that the Goodman/Perls model, taken literally, tends to do. Thus again, the "retroflection" process of inhibiting one urge in favor of another, or acting on or for oneself rather than with others, at a given moment, is not a *resistance to contact* but *is* the contact, or is one functional mode or aspect of the contact, at a given moment, under given conditions.

All this unclarity is greatly alleviated by giving up the notion that contact is one thing, and retroflection, say, is another, opposed thing. Crossing or meeting some "external" boundary (interpersonal or just "environmental"), and not crossing it (retroflection), become simply two possible contact modes—or better, two poles of the modulation of the contact function of *exchange* (where contact, again, is defined comprehensively as the organization of the self in the field). The *evaluation* of the operation of that function, again, is sought in its relationship to the goals of the subject, in relation to the conditions of the field. Thus, the degree or exercise of retroflective style by a salesperson may be evaluated differently from that of a scholar, that of a doctor from that of a cloistered monk—but we still may have the healthy exercise of all these activities, by healthy people, with the differing kinds and amounts of retroflection appropriate in each situation. This is by contrast to the Perls/Goodman quotation cited above, which would seem to suggest that a life choice of, say, celibacy, is inherently less acceptable, less healthy, than another choice. But this would seem to reintroduce the kind of "extrinsic standards" in the study of personal process that Goodman, in particular, so roundly criticized in the psychodynamic approach, and was intent on avoiding in his own model.

The same thing can then be said, clearly, for each of the other "resistances,"—or for that matter for each of the avoidances or functions (or pairs of functions) in the long list gleaned from Perls above. In each case, as discussed in chapter IV, the Cleveland School has been at pains to point out, quite rightly, the creative, adaptive, and even necessary aspects of these "resistances to contact"—thus leaving us in a theoretical quandary about when is a resistance a resistance, and when not. Goodman, as we have seen, attempted to sidestep this difficulty by tying the "resistance," however creative and even desirable, to "repressions in the field" (Perls et al., 1951, p. 522). This Freudian cast to the argument, as we have seen, while advancing the terms of discussion beyond simple "chewing" to the more complexly organized concept "awareness," still does not answer the objection here, that there can be no "contact"—no "chewing," no "aware behavior," and no "organization of the self in the field" at all—that does not consist of these same functional processes, which were labeled as resistances.

In sum, our argument here is that there is no such thing as a "resistance to contact." There may be "resistances to awareness," but these themselves, as outlined above (in the discussion of repression, for example) *are* a form of contact. What there are, are different and infinitely varying ways of *organizing the self in the field* which is to say, varieties of contact, which are made up of the modulation of all the various polar *modes* or *functions* of contact which can be seen to be relevant (or inimical, possibly) to the purposes and the field at hand. And there are, correspondingly, various degrees or kinds of success of contact, or products of contact, or types of contact possible, given those modes, under those purposes and in that field. In other words, the various *organizations* produced may still be evaluated, by the subject himself or by a change agent or other observer, in terms of what those goals are—or even conceivably what they "should be"—of the contact itself. And again, all of this should still be just as true whether the "subject" in question is an individual, or an organized system of individuals of some kind—a couple, a family, a group, a work system, a society. In all cases alike, the evaluation of functioning, of contact by all these various and varying modes, follows from consideration of goals of the system (and again, of the interaction of that system, those goals with the limiting or enabling conditions in the field).

Now as we have said, the larger the system, the more the goals may seem to vary, from one case to another. All systems may have common goals of survival and self-perpetuation, and this commonality may seem to dictate certain universal necessities of contact function. But within this, the variation of goals and styles, and thus the evaluation of appropriate behavior and function, between and among, say, an automaker, a municipal government, a consulting firm, a social club, a PAC, and a health clinic, will be enormous. All must have some functional resistance and some functional confluence—or else, as argued above, they would soon cease to exist as defined entities with boundaries at all. But beyond this, their contact styles—that is, their particular mix or map of contact functions appropriate or "healthy" for their particular goals— will necessarily and healthily vary widely, just as their goals and contexts do. To attempt to diagnose organizations in terms of a standard list of "resistances to contact" (as Brown & Merry do, 1987), is, we would argue, to introduce an unnecessary and even confusing step in the diagnostic process—a step of evaluation in a descriptive stage of the diagnostic process itself, and one that then has to be undone so that the work of planning intervention can proceed. That is, having characterized the organization in question in terms of its "resistances" (which is of course already an evaluation, an implication of a dysfunctional departure from some ideal contact state), then the same diagnostic process must back up and say that, after all, some "resistances" may be functional and even necessary, or at any rate acceptable and unavoidable, depending on the nature of the activity, so that work can get done. This is equivalent to the Harris statement above, quoted by Zinker (and very much in the Freudian spirit of seeing the "defenses" as inevitable, if tragic, compromises with one's true nature), that retroflection is the mark of civilization. We would rather say it is the mark of existence, of self-maintenance as an independent entity—and not, as the Goodman/Perls formulation implies, that there is some ideal, state-of-nature "contact" that is *not* tarnished or compromised by retroflective elements (or deflective, or confluent, or differentiating/resistant, and so forth). Returning to the diagnosis of organizations, why describe them in extrinsically loaded terms of "resistance" at all in the first place, if only to turn around and take the evaluative characterization back (and somewhat lamely, we are contending here)? Why not make the description in terms of functional considerations in the first place, and then evaluate which functions contribute to the achievement of organizational goals and which ones introduce an unncessary cost or block to that "contact"—and which functions ("resistances") may be missing altogether, that are needed for better functioning? Certainly this is what Merry and Brown and other successful consultants do in the end anyway (see again, for example, E. Nevis, 1987, p. 64)—just as it was argued above that skilled therapists working under the Gestalt paradigm were already treating resistance and ground in the general ways outlined here, against the grain, so to speak, of the received theory. A good theory (to return to Lewin) must be above all an effective guide to action, or else it was not a successful description of structure and process in the first place. The argument here is not that successful practicioners, of individuals therapy or of organization consultation either one, should change their way of working to conform to this theoretical revision—but rather that successful change agents are already working this way, and the theory needs revision to a new level of internal congruence to conform to *them* (again, see E. Nevis, 1987, for descriptions of consultant work, albeit from a somewhat different angle, that are very much in harmony with the revisions offered here).

Once again, everything that we have been saying about the institutional or multiperson case should apply to the individual "system" case as well. The goal of the individual, as elegantly derived by Goodman (Perls, et al., 1951, p. 270), following Goldstein and anticipating Maslow, is *growth*. This follows from the terms of the Gestalt conception of context and boundary in the first place: contact at the boundary is by definition with something "other" than the self, something that can be absorbed/assimilated/incorporated (whether literally or cognitively, as information). But this assimilation itself can never be merely a passive, additive process. Rather, it is the "creative adjustment" of the organism to the new conditions, the new material (and vice versa)—what we have been calling the (re)organization of the self in the field, as our definition of contact. Here again, our only quarrel with Goodman is over his tendency, growing out of understandable reformist zeal, to emphasize one pole, one dimension of this whole contact, at the expense of the other. That is, we would say, in the spirit of everything above, that the *goal* of the "organism," the purpose of the contact, is to balance or integrate *growth* (or change) with *conservation* (which is to say, with ongoing structures of ground). *Both* poles are essential for the contact to take place and to continue. There can be no growth without conservation, because there would be nothing to grow "on to"; change without a considerable element of conservation might just as well turn out to be a net loss, and not a growth at all (sadly, analogies abound in cases of psychotherapy-gone-wrong). Nor can there be conservation without growth, without assimilation/accommodation and reorganization around the new material—because without this "feeding" process, the organism soon dies (and here we can see as well the intuitive rightness of Perls's attempt, however theoretically incomplete, to link the metaphors of figure/ground and of eating processes, as descriptive images of organic functioning). Conservation and growth are the fundamental, inherent poles, or polar dimensions, of contact—just as "resistance/differentiation" and "confluence," or "deflection/selectivity" and something we might call "openness," are. To emphasize only the one (growth) without giving corresponding weight to the other (conservation), as Goodman does, is, again, to distort "contact" itself, equating it only with change— and then idealizing the "contact/change" process while disparaging "resistances to contact/change," with all the resultant distortions in the model discussed down through this chapter.

To be sure, as Goodman argues in his presentation, if an individual cannot grow and change, the result is rigidity, "dis-passion," anhedonia, grayness, anomie, living death or death itself, the endless repetition of isolated gestures that have lost context and meaning. But by the same token, if the individual cannot conserve, while changing, cannot organize the new into enduring meaningful structures (of ground), the result will be the "contact junkie," exhibiting, ironically, all the same symptoms, the same anomie, the same repetition of endless acts-in-isolation, with only the difference that the ritualized gesture here is the rigid insistence on seeming novelty in place of the rigid insistence on seeming sameness above. Novelty and sameness, *pace* Goodman, can amount to the same series of elements in isolation, unless they are organized/integrated into some ongoing structures of ground, which supply meaning to figure—which is to say, into a *conservative* structure (i.e., one with enduring organization over time), which can nevertheless change by the incorporation of new material, yet without a break in the continuity of identity. And once more, we would emphasize that these principles have to apply equally to individual and to multipersonal systems or cases.

In other words, we are now arriving at a model of "organismic" functioning which—whatever its capacities and powers—can apply those capacities diagnostically and prescriptively to both individual and multiperson systems equally. Leaving aside for the moment the question of what exactly those capacities are, at the very least we can say that such a "dual" or multilevel model would be an extremely interesting and useful tool to have. As mentioned in Chapter IV, movement across this "boundary" between individual and "systems" perspectives has proved to be a particularly tricky task for various clinical models attempting to generalize upward (the psychodynamic model in particular comes to mind)—while the various social psychology models, which may tell us a great many interesting things about social role, membership, group behavior, attitude formation, and attributional phenomena, do not directly address questions we want to raise about *organization of the self* or personality dynamics in the familiar sense.

And yet, there are so many cases where the ability to describe and diagnose the individual and the social system (couple, family, organization, and so forth) *in the same terminology* is the very thing we want to be able to do—or would want to do, if only the very difficulty of doing so did not act to inhibit contextual approaches to individual problems in the first place. The problem manager *in the problem organization*, the problem child in the problem classroom, the "identified patient" in the problem family—even the problem citizen in the problem community—all of these are cases "at the boundary," so to speak, between consultation and therapy, or else are cases which are artificially forced, by the lack of a common language at different levels, into one side or the other of the too-rigid boundary between these levels (which results in turn from that very absence of common terms).

This model, which results from combining the renewed consideration of structured ground with the revised conception of "resistance" developed through the foregoing chapters, might begin with a mapping, or functional tabulation, of all the relevant (bipolar) contact functions of the given system under examination (individual or multipersonal), with a view to determining, first of all, a description of its functional contact *style*—i.e., the subjective topography or structured ground in which "figures of contact" (or goals) are generated, energized, achieved, and then integrated (or not integrated) into ongoing functioning and higher-level goals. The "relevant contact functions," again, at least in the organizational case, are given by the goals/activities of the system itself, together with consideration of environmental features—available resources, pressures, constraints, and so forth. (In the individual case, again, there is no objection under this approach to starting with some "standard" list of relevant personal contact functions for consideration, such as are given by Goodman, Perls, the Polsters, Zinker, or other writers in the field—*as long as* the listing includes both poles of each of these contact *modes*, resistance/differentiation *and* confluence, growth *and* conservation, retroflection *and* expression/dependency.) How this "topological" or functional mapping model then plays out in practice, and what kinds of diagnosis and prescription are facilitated by this approach, will be taken up in the case study chapters that follow.

Finally, it should be emphasized that this approach to diagnosis and change, which emphasizes *ongoing structures and functional patterns of organization*, is by no means intended to replace or contradict the well-established Cleveland model of diagnosis of systemic functioning by reference to the Experience Cycle. On the contrary, the two approaches, far from being contradictory, are complementary to each other, in yet another example of bipolar dimensions in contact. The Cycle model, as a diagnostic/prescriptive tool, is a still-photography or "snapshot" approach to systems analysis (again, whether on the individual or group level)—the anatomy of an impulse in isolation, as an exemplary case for study, without an extended time dimension but obviously in the hope of revealing characteristic dysfunctions (or strengths) that apply across situations and over time. Our criticism of that model, as lending itself too easily to an "episodic" or "impulse-in-series" view of functioning, would apply only to the exclusive use of that penetrating diagnostic tool, without reference to ongoing structures of ground. At that point, the tool and the model would become "figure-bound," in all the ways discussed above. But the usefulness of the Cleveland model, by these arguments, is enhanced, not diminished or eliminated, by reintroduction of the "missing polar function" of diagnosis in the more traditional sense, which is the analysis proposed here of those *stable ground features of contact functioning* which are institutionalized in the life of the person or system, and organized dynamically/hierarchically over time, along the lines developed here.

With that said, let us turn in the final chapters to a more concrete application of all these arguments, and this revised model, in two sets of actual cases. In particular we will be trying to trace the relationship and interaction between these two polar approaches in application, the practical choice points within and between them, and the capacity of the new model promised above to move flexibly and productively "up" and "down" the various levels of a human problem, in a social context.

The Structure of Ground:
Two Clinical Cases

THE CASE OF JOSH, OR SCYLLA AND CHARYBDIS

WHEN the hero Odysseus was wending his long way homeward after the fiasco of the Trojan War—an involved family drama that had already cost him his youth and most of his friends, and now threatened three generations of his own household—a goddess appeared to him in a dream to warn of further dangers ahead. His way would lie, she foretold, along a narrow channel between two headlands, both guarded by monsters. In the high cliffs to one side lurked the harpy Scylla, ready to swoop from her nest and snatch her prey six at a time, one for each horrible gullet, from the deck of any vessel that strayed too close to her shore. Worse, on the opposite bank lay Charybdis, the whirlpool, with open maw to suck down anything that came in reach, men and ships and all.

133

Set your course for Scylla, the goddess counseled, row hard, and take your punishment. Better to lose six, or even twelve, and press on, diminished but still alive, than sink forever into the maelstrom in one final backward suicidal dissolve.

It was Josh himself who first drew the parallel between his own life and the old story—that looming image of twin figures of danger, damned if you do and damned if you don't, that everybody experiences at one moment or another in life, generally in less drastic metaphors like Hobson's choice, or lying between a rock and a hard place. The difference for Josh was that this was not just figure: it was also ground. This stance, this way of approaching the world, was, to use the familiar Gestalt phrase, Josh's existence. His life was mapped, to continue the traveler's analogy, onto that narrow space between two catastrophes—and then the whole image held frozen with the support of a liberal fixative solution of alcohol.

Scylla, for Josh, was the agonizing, self-consuming guilt he experienced whenever he asked for anything for himself, however modest and appropriate the self-assertion might seem (the polarity of inappropriate, out-of-touch entitlements was of course another matter, such as the pattern of spending three weekends out of four in a drunken stupor, with occasional binges in between). Even the very fact of being listened to was potentially catastrophic to Josh, since at best this would represent time and attention and possibly sympathetic nourishment snatched from somebody else (meaning, by definition, somebody more deserving). At worst, Josh's fears took on a darkly magical quality, as if today's complaint, the present hint of the volcano of hurt and grief and anger he carried inside, could magically reach back in time and destroy the fragile mother he had labored his whole life to prop up and protect.

The roots of this side of his dilemma were not hard to trace in the ground of Josh's personal history. The oldest of four closely-spaced siblings, Josh grew up as principal caretaker to a family of financially affluent but emotionally starving children, including two child-adults. His father was alcoholic, workaholic, probably schizoid, constantly on the road as a highly successful salesman, or if at home, then invariably, in Josh's image, drunk on the sofa in front of the TV, from which command post he barked savage orders that nobody paid any attention to, least of all the string of ineffectual housekeepers that came and went, but mostly went, through the endless, unchanging years of Josh's childhood. His mother, a fragile, narcissistic, depressive woman, probably addicted to a whole array of prescription drugs, was frequently hospitalized for one complaint or another, or if at home, then generally in her own room in another part of the house, lights out and shades drawn. This pattern worsened after the birth of each successive child, particularly the second son, who was diagnosed as having significant developmental delays. By the age of six, Josh felt, and to a large extent no doubt was, in charge of the whole household, sometimes to the point of actually being alone in the house with three younger siblings, with only the uncertain assistance of a three-year-old sister. In the pattern we discussed in Chapter IV as retroflection-II, Josh tried to supply the stable parenting and supportive ground he so desperately needed by being that parent and that ground himself for the other children—something he was to repeat, years later, in his work life, where he "mother-henned" his own supervisory charges to the point of infantilization, with predictably mixed results.

One of the many costs of this organization of self, this contact approach or structure, then and later, was the tidal wave of panic and guilt mentioned above that loomed over Josh if ever he seemed to assert or accept the right to a bit of direct nourishment for himself. (The bottle he sucked so avidly, at intervals, was again another matter. Any organization of self, in our sense here, is by definition overdetermined, and one element of that overdetermination for Josh was supplied by a dream image of a deranged and frantic mother, keeping the household poisons out of the hands of the children by drinking them all her/himself. And indeed, strangely and wonderfully, none of Josh's siblings had grown up to be a substance abuser; all, including the "retarded" brother, were employed, married, and apparently stable, independent people. And still Josh kept trying to soak up all the poison!) In therapy, this terror of the guilt-harpy took the form of a rigid insistence on preventive self-flagellation. I must promise, Josh demanded in the first session, to focus always and exclusively on his own short-comings and demerits, like the series of "alcohol counselors," in his description, that he had seen in the past. Anything else would be a copout. He and only he was responsible for his drinking, his failure to do more for his own wife and children, and his general lack of responsibility—which only goes to show how anything, even a caricatured "Gestalt" autonomy, can be used as a "resistance," in the traditional sense, to responsibility itself, and to change! Certainly Josh was autonomous: in the midst of his highly competent (and highly "enabling" or codependent) wife and three very active small children, he lived alone. And I must be quick about it! Like the proverbial state of nature, proper therapy in Josh's view was "nasty, brutish, and short." Only thus could he justify the expenditure of money, which of course could have been better spent on some much worthier object. And more importantly, only thus could he *organize the contact between us,* which threatened to stir the Scylla of guilt, hovering always over his head.

Now clearly, an interesting and possibly implosive Gestalt approach to Josh's impasse might be built around work with this overwhelming figure of guilt, entering it, exploring it, and making it the subject of experiment—whether formally, or more naturalistically, in a conversational format. Josh might sharpen his awareness of himself-as-victim, and from there he might begin to make contact with Josh-as-Scylla, the harpy introject he carried always with him, and in whose shadow he lived. And from there, a new mobilization of energy, a new creative adjustment might form and flow. If I did not choose to go directly down this road with Josh, it was first of all because of my sense that, for him, *the figure was stale.* How to find a new purchase, a new sense of urgent reality, in that obsessively punitive figure he had lived with in sharp if rigid relief now for thirty-some-odd years? Zinker, Fantz, Perls himself, and perhaps others as well might have done it; I was not at all sure I could support Josh to find the way. More particularly, I could not feel my way to freshness, to something new with and for Josh, given his demonstrated talent for taking each new insight, each potential support, and using it for further self-punishment in his own retroflective, isolated, and all-too-autonomous way.

The new thing for Josh, it seemed to me, was the very fact of being there in the room *with me*—a contact problem he was already working frantically to structure in the familiar terms of his own organized ground, which is to say in terms of the map (and phrasebook) he was calling "alcohol counseling," a repetitive script in which he would demand nothing of me, I would demand nothing of him (except for the ritual self-flagellation), and the whole relationship would be channeled—anger, heartbreak, understanding and misunderstanding, humor, love, eroticism, and whatever else might come up—through the narrow and stylized language of punishment and blame. But I was not an "alcohol counselor." For whatever reason—the contact demands of his growing children, his wife's threats to leave him, the chafing rigidity of his creative adjustment or self-organization itself—he had come to somebody different, presumably for something new. I took a deep breath and told Josh I could not agree to his terms. In the first place, I told him, I had no idea what an "alcohol counselor" was; I only counseled people, not bottles, and besides, since he obviously knew a lot more about drinking than I did, it seemed absurd for him to spend his time and money getting me to counsel him about it. In the second place, I could not agree with his notions about autonomy. I had never met the mythical person he was describing, who was totally and exclusively responsible for himself, I said, and I couldn't imagine what such a freak would look like. In my view, people were co-responsible for each other, as well as themselves, even if there are certain things each of us can only decide, in the end, for ourselves (with the individual figure of choice, in our language here, growing out of a mutual ground of support). In his case, if I got to know him and care about him, and came to hear about people that had hurt him, now or in the past, no way could I promise in advance never to feel angry or even blaming toward those people, however distressing that might be to him. Josh looked at me like I was a Martian, but at the part about counseling him on how to drink, he smiled broadly. At that, I relaxed—a little. In my own personal organization of self-in-contact, if the shared ground includes the possibility of teasing and being teased, then I feel freed up. In case of hard relational times, the mutual ground structure of joining-through-humor will be there, at least sometimes, at least potentially, at moments when other contact organizations fail.

The second reason for not going with the figure of guilt that Josh presented so strongly, besides the question of freshness, was my sense from the first of a second ongoing figure, or ground structure (since a figure that endures over time becomes a structure of ground), equal in size and weight to the first but hovering in shadow behind it, not yet clearly seen or articulated by either of us. This, as Josh was later to express it so vividly, was Charybdis the undertow, guardian of the opposite shore, whose other name was shame. If self-assertion, self-advertisement, or (nonself)-blame aroused debilitating bouts of guilt in Josh, the opposite extreme, of self-abnegation, isolation, and silence, left him in an earlier and even more desperate position, which was a flood of shame. And earlier, as the developmental models tell us, means worse, in the sense of more fundamentally organizing, and more potentially destructive. Indeed, the self psychologists are teaching us to think that it is shame, not guilt, that operates in most suicides—that organizes the ground, in our language, from which suicide can move, as a figure, from awareness to mobilization to action (see for example Morrison, 1987). Guilt, after all, is a strong feeling, if a negative one, and one very much connected with other people: one has done something, or not done something, by definition, *to* someone. Shame, by contrast, is weak, deeply private—in a word, shameful; so much so that, as Nathanson has pointed out (1987), until quite recently it has been little discussed in clinical literature. One can proclaim one's guilt (whole cultural styles have been built on this proposition); one is ashamed of one's shame. Guilt can be expiated, directly or indirectly; shame leads one to hide—with suicide as the ultimate figure of hiding. "Go for the guilt," was the laconic counsel of a senior psychotherapist I consulted informally, as Josh and I together began to understand the structures of his ground. Praying that she, and the goddess, and my own clinical intuition were all right, I steered, with Josh, for the cliff shore, and tried to stay with him, through the storms and (self)-depredations that ensued.

This, then, became our first therapeutic experiment—within the context of the wider experimental ground, of being in the room together, person to person, at all. For weeks I listened with a heavy heart to Josh's story as it poured out, spurning or ignoring his frequent, sometimes desperate attempts to turn the conversation back to the safe structured track of his usual outpouring of quite another kind, alone in his basement den at home on the weekends, bottle in hand—laughing when Josh laughed, crying when he cried, outraged and angry when Josh denied or couldn't find those feelings in his own ground, purposely letting my jaw hang open in shock or dismay at the things Josh had never questioned, even managing to tease him a little at times, perhaps through tears on both our faces, at the byzantine contortions he would put himself through to avoid including his own child self within the compass of his own universal human compassion and concern. Josh was politically concerned and actively engaged in charitable causes, social action, brotherhood, and saving the children. Only one child, it seemed, was so singularly underserving, in all the world, as to be singled out for exclusion from the otherwise boundless largesse of his heart. At this Josh would laugh ruefully, and cry again.

Punctuating these catharses, through all this initial period, in and out of the sessions, was the recurrent cycle of self-condemnation and recrimination Josh put himself through, for the indulgence, the outrageous self-centeredness, the fatal self-aggrandizement of his own bids for sympathy, manipulative in his mind, and his own emerging feelings of blame. And again, I held back from taking and "working" these figures of punishment and anger, both for the sake of pushing ahead with the fresh figure of the contact between us and to continue building the ground for the stirrings of Charybdis yet to come. When Josh railed at himself for wasting the therapy hour in a wallow of self-pity, I protested the exclusion vehemently. After all, I was there too, and at least as responsible for wasting the session as he was. If there was blame to be dealt out, I insisted on getting my share; anything less, I told him, would be deeply insulting and I wouldn't stand for it. When Josh laughed and cried foul for using sophistry to put him in a logical bind, I told him the only bind he was in was what he was going to do with me, given that I couldn't stand to be left out. When he ventured, ever so cautiously, to suggest that that sounded just a teeny bit egocentric, I told him that unlike alcohol, here we had a topic I knew something about and could give him tips on, any time. Then fresh paroxysms of self-reproach for having breathed a hint of criticism of me, after all my caring, and all my long-suffering toleration of him (and was I wrong to hear the first rumblings of Charybdis in this emerging characterization of himself as not just guilty but actually toxic? No wonder he felt the best thing he could do for his children was to keep away from them—again a chain of figures whose logical extreme is suicide).

And so it went. Around this time Josh had a dream—one of the first he allowed himself to remember and bring in as he gradually destructured some of the rigid boundaries of his own personal ground, to admit the possibility of the presence of another person on intimate terrain. In his dream he was out walking with his little daughter, first in a stroller and then in a backpack, both of them clearly marked with the familiar baby-supply company logo, "Gerry Co." A driver in a passing car swerved to miss another pedestrian, threatening to hit Josh and the baby on the sidewalk.

"Blow your horn!" Josh screamed wildly, while simultaneously reflecting on the oddity of trying to warn himself. The driver did, and Josh leaped back, and they were safe. The horn, however, was stuck, and continued to blare, louder and louder, until houses and buildings around began to crumble. Finally not one stone was left standing on another—"like Armageddon," Josh commented in the retelling—and he and his child were left standing alone, surrounded by a sea of rubble. He woke up deeply rattled, considered starting to drink before breakfast, remembered he was coming to therapy, and decided he would give that a try first. Then, if he was still shaking, he could always call in sick, stay home, and drink all day.

Now they say that Freudian patients dream Freudian dreams, Jungian patients dream animas and archetypes, and so forth. Certainly, for what it is worth, my clients dream puns and anagrams, in great number—or so at any rate it always seems to me. First of all I told Josh, drawing on the inspired formulation offered by Isadore From (who with characteristic modesty attempts to pass the credit on to Rank; see Wysong & Rosenfeld, 1982, p. 38), that the dream, seeing as how he remembered it so vividly and brought it in so purposefully, must contain, among other things, *a message for me, or for us, about our work together, or a comment of some kind about the ground of relationship between us.* What did he make, I asked, of the label on the baby carrier? "What—Gerryco?" Josh asked, running it together for the first time out loud; and then, visibly shaken now, "You mean—Jericho?"

"Is that how it feels?" I asked, but it wasn't really a question. "But I don't blow my own horn," Josh replied slowly. "No, you don't," I agreed. "But maybe there's a reckless driver in this room that we've been letting do it for you."

The dream, as another example of overdetermined organization, has many levels. Personal and social, inner and outer worlds, are, as Goodman has taught us, among the many false dichotomies, precipitates of a wrong understanding of awareness, that the Gestalt perspective can address and heal. If it is certainly true, in the traditional Gestalt view, that the "dreamer plays all the parts," which is to say that the organization of the inner world is mapped onto the environment in the dream, then it is equally true that the outer, social world, people and relationships and feelings about them, are mapped into the inner world of the same dream. In Josh's case, once again, I judged it was more lively, and more urgent in view of the probable storms ahead, to work from the relationship, as the more nelgected, more *pregnant* pole (in Wertheimer's sense of *praegnanz*—see Chapter I), of this unified, organized awareness field. If walls were tumbling down for this Joshua, opening new possibilities for contact, there was also the potentially dangerous loss of necessary structures of ground, without which no contact, by our argument throughout these chapters, is even possible. This then was the cost, at least possibly, of my own choice of a pushy, "hot," emphatically interpersonal contact strategy with Joshua: namely, that the process, being in some sense led by me, might be speeding out of control for Josh, leaving him alone in an empty field of the shards of his former contact structures—or worse than alone, since once again he was put in the position, with the dream baby, of a caretaker without resources. Homeopathic to the end, I could see no way out of this impasse except more of the same medicine (and in all fairness, we should note that the same thing, an out-of-control destructuring of ground, might easily happen with a more intrapersonal approach): in other words, Charybdis must be brought into the session, and into the relationship, from her stalking ground at home with Josh alone, in the wee hours of the night.

Did I think it was a good dream, Josh queried? The best, I pronounced: clear, poetic, beautiful. The only thing was, I told him, how about if next time he tried letting the driver of the car stay there with him, after everything crumbled. It was not the first time Josh looked at me with that particular mixture of suspicion and disbelief, as if to say that if he was unhappy, at least he wasn't crazy, which was better than the other way around.

Meanwhile, Josh's bouts with shame, medicated and possibly worsened by alcohol in the dark night watches, were growing more intense—or perhaps he was just making more references to them. My suggestion that he might consider giving me a call sometime during one of these attacks of despair was greeted with predictable outrage and preventive guilt (and considerably more freedom of expression than a few months back). "Don't you know *anything*?" he demanded in fury. "How naive can you *get*? Don't you understand that I am an *alcoholic*. If I'm feeling that way, I drink, and if I'm drunk, you'd be talking to a bottle, not a person. So I'd be waking you up at four in the morning for nothing."

I said we wouldn't know the results of the experiment until

we tried it, that all he would get at four in the morning would be the answering machine, which he was welcome to use—but that at ten or eleven or even twelve in the evening, he might get me, and he might use the occasion to tell me things on his heart and mind at that hour that were harder to feel or say in the morning. In that way, I told him, if alcohol served to support the ongoing contact and exploration between us, then by all means we should consider taking advantage of it. Then followed the customary irate lecture about how I understodd nothing about alcoholism or alcohol counseling, whatever else I might know—and that seemingly I was unteachable to boot. After this particular outburst Josh came in the next session to tell me he had suddenly realized he had failed to apologize for blowing up at me, for the first time, and what was more, he hadn't even remembered to feel guilty over it in the meantime. His comment took me by surprise; rightly or wrongly I attempted for once with Josh to hide the sudden misting in my eyes at this small, unimaginable victory, for fear of jointly owning it away from his new, appropriate autonomy. "That's what you want, isn't it," Josh remarked quietly, after an intense look. "Let's just say, it frees me up, for more fighting," I replied. And together we passed a tender moment.

Parenthetically, one of our ongoing and noisier battles continued to be over the word "alcoholic" itself, which is an exceedingly tricky term from a Gestalt perspective. To the extent that "alcoholism" is meant to refer to a disease, in the ordinary medical sense, and not just a pattern of behavior, it raises questions of projection, introjection, and possession, in the germ- or dybbuk-theory sense. Since the evidence for biochemical addiction or addictive propensity to alcohol is scanty and contradictory, the disease model, with its seeming separation of person and agency so foreign to the Gestalt view of health and nature, must remain highly problematic, at best, from a Gestalt point of view. In the traditional AA model, things become even more convoluted, since the same person who is exhorted, with the support of interpersonal and spiritual ground structures, to have agency or "will power" over the first drink in any given drinking sequence, is also presumed to lose that agency instantly and entirely after that first dose. Obviously, such a perspective might lend itself to self-fulfilling prophecy. Clearly, the AA network and perspective are a supportive and reorganizing force in the lives of many people. At the same time it may be that there are others, like or unlike Josh, who may feel paralyzed or shamed by the depersonalized aspects of the traditional AA approach, or who may use the "helpless victim" (of one's own chemistry, seemingly) perspective to rigidify, rather than destructure, a destructive behavior pattern. Clearly, there is much useful and potentially clarifying Gestalt work to be done in this area. Meantime, with Josh I continued doggedly to use the term "overdrinking"—which continued to provoke and infuriate him, by disturbing his own particular blend of exaggeration and denial of personal responsibility, and his habitual interplay of guilt versus shame. (For a related treatment of the terminology topic from a non-Gestalt viewpoint, see Fingarette, 1988.)

Now in everything that had passed between us up to this point, clearly much of what I had been trying to do with Josh was to discourage or destructure a transferential relationship, in the Freudian sense, such as he had had, to some extent, with his previous "alcohol counselors." Josh's problem, as I understood it, was a severely constricted *contact style*—which is to say ground structure or organization of self in the field—which held him in an extremely isolated position. In view of that, and in view of his skill at turning new relationships into repetitions of old ones—i.e., recasting the new figure in terms of rigid ground structures—a transferential approach, it seemed to me, would be more likely to solidify than to destructure Josh's "walls." Thus I had preferred, following Goodman and Perls (Perls et al., 1951, e.g., p. 293), to insist on developing the present relationship, in all its painful and surprising reality, both figure and accumulating ground—and on making this development and this relationship the main subject and the main experiment of the therapy. But again, this did carry risks, perhaps more so than a classic or transferential approach, of destructuring Josh's "defenses" (to use that language) faster than the organization of new structures, new contact possibilities, could arise to take their place. And as we have seen, this might be true whether one followed a "figure" approach, as in the traditional Gestalt model, or a "ground" emphasis, as here.

Other perspectives have their own contributions to make to an understanding of what was going on between us, and within Josh (which again, echoing Goodman, must in some sense be the same thing). From a self-psychology point of view, much of what I had been doing, even some of the differentiation and arguing, could be seen as that process of *empathic mirroring* which Kohut sees as the beginnings of formation of self—and the lack of which leads to narcissistic isolation for want of healthy links to the world (in his terminology, mature self-objects, where "self-object" is understood as the polar complement to our process concept of projection. That is, where projection, in the Gestalt view, is the identifying of part of the self as belonging to the environment, outside the self boundary, "self-object" is that part of the environment which is experienced as within the boundary of the self; Kohut, 1977).

Similarly, from an object-relations point of view, we could say that the therapeutic process thus far had been one of establishing *containment* (in our language, relational ground) of Josh's affect, experience, and experimental extensions of self (see for example Winnicott, 1988). In Winnicott's famous phrasing, the affective or empathic response need not be perfect (indeed, from a Gestalt point of view, such an absence of differentiation would in itself raise serious problems of identity diffusion and loss of autonomy for the client), but need only be *good enough* for the client to be able and willing to continue the inherently rewarding experiment of interpersonal exploration, or contact. To the early Perls, Josh's early development would have undergone a distortion, whether from introjection of a negative self-description (Sullivan's "bad me,") or a confluence, or simply an absence of caretakers—all of them leading to inhibition of healthy, aggressive self-assertion, and to a resultant "short-circuiting" of aggressive contact with the environment, through the mechanism or resistance of retroflection. To this Goodman would have added that the attentive focus on figure formation and figure destruction would have inherently self-corrective effects, leading by means of the natural tendency of the organism toward health, to a more inclusive creative adjustment and a more passionate figure of contact. And the Cleveland School would tell us how to go about that process of attentive focusing, where to break down and analyze the figure-formation process itself, and the meaning of the various possible interruptions or distortions, as well as how to construct active experiments to address those characteristic breakdown points.

To all of these rich and varied perspectives, by no means mutually contradictory in themselves, we would only add two things: one, *that at least in some cases, the most lively and preg-*

nant figure for study is the nascent and ongoing relationship in the room itself; and two, *that a full and useful understanding of figure formation and figure destruction is enhanced by—indeed, is incomplete without—direct consideration of ongoing structures of ground,* both the given intrapersonal ground of the client, and the developing interpersonal ground, of the two therapeutic partners themselves. In contact terms, under the arguments developed all through these pages, this means that we will view preferred or possible contact patterns, which is to say structures of that ground, not just as "resistances" to an ideal contact process, but as the means or strategies by which a particular figure of contact is developed and achieved, both intra- and interpersonally. (One is tempted to say here that this represents a shift, all through these chapters, from Goodman-the-Platonic-idealist to Goodman-the-Aristotelian-empiricist and social psychologist—since certainly he contained and expressed both of these polar themes, sometimes, by our arguments here, in an unintegrated way). In Josh's case, this meant, for example, choosing to regard even alcohol itself, in its function as part of a larger retroflective and desensitizing system, as not only a block or resistance to overwhelmingly chaotic or disorganized contact (a contradiction in terms, in this view), but also as part of an overall strategy and support for organizing and thus permitting the kinds and degrees of contact that Josh himself imagined and experienced as possible.

To be sure, there is a paradoxical element in all this, since the act of joining a retroflective or desensitized system must perforce have a destructuring and possibly reorganizing effect on that system—an approach which was carried in this case, as we have just been discussing, to the extreme of inviting the client to share, in a sense, even his drinking bouts themselves with the therapist (with the obvious caveat that only one of us was drinking—a structural difference in relational ground in the therapy which is also represented by the payment of a fee). Still, the theoretical argument of this exposition, particularly as developed in Chapter V, has been all along that *no* contact, no organization of self in the field, no resolution of figure and structured ground is possible without some strategic provision for both retroflection and desensitization among other functional necessities. It is the particular insight and contribution of our Gestalt point of view, handed down from Goodman and Perls, that therapeutic change flows from *go-*

ing to the contact that is possible and that the complex interpersonal intervention of joining-and-analyzing that contact process, *thereby destructuring it*, unblocks the rich and spontaneous possibility of a new and more satisfying creative adjustment, a new organization of self in the field. Once again, what we would add or clarify in that perspective here is that gestalt formation means a resolution of figure *and* ground, in terms of each other; that that ground resolution is itself highly structured and enduring over time; and that our understanding of contact and of our clients is enhanced by direct attention to those ground structures.

In Josh's ground, the sleeping but ever-menacing figure of shame, which he had called Charybdis, was beginning to wake and stir. As he began to share the panic and horror of this experience more and more with me—in a lengthy chaotic period of late-night calls, and hurt feelings over my self-protective call-screening (and guilt about those calls that did get through)—a fuller picture of the ground of his existence gradually emerged, and a fuller joining, at times as painful as touching a raw wound, could begin to occur. Developmentally speaking, this was the move back from the guilty sibling, who perhaps wished death on competing hungry mouths in a shortage economy, to the self-loathing and self-abandonment of the infant who could not command Kohut's empathic mirroring, or Winnicott's empathic holding, from his absent and distracted mother. Josh's risk of suicide, active or passive, was much greater in this period in my judgment (and in his), and much therapeutic time was spent on the careful and sometimes combative negotiation of contracts—about driving, about mixing pills and alcohol, about calling, about what to do when calls to me did not go through. For the sake of my own life needs and in consideration of Josh's guilt structures and autonomy issues, I could not be available to him twenty-four hours a day—a familiar problem to therapists in private practice, without round-the-clock emergency clinical support. Often he threatened to leave therapy. Once I threatened to come to his home if he missed a session, ring his bell, and bill him as usual (a Lacanian figure, I hasten to add, that I would never offer against the ground of a different client, with a different organization of commitment, ambivalence, and relationship). Once he told me he had driven halfway to my house at 4:00 A.M., but had turned back at the thought of how angry I would be—not, he said with a smile, because he thought I would kick him out of therapy, but because he knew I wouldn't, and then he'd have to hear about it "for the rest of my life." (At this point, obviously, Josh assumed therapy would last forever.)

As the structured ground of Josh's life began to undergo re-organization, new figures of contact became possible. Over the next few years he quit his job, took a degree in hospital administration, and achieved a new integration of his management skills and his desire to take care of others. Even more importantly, he began to talk to and play with his own children, who had been shadowy figures to him up to this point, always dealt with indirectly through his wife (so as to protect them from noxious contact). In the process, he discovered at least a few ways to relive the childhood he had never known—even recapturing, in the process, long-forgotten memories of hilarious romping with his little sisters and his "re-tarded" brother, sometimes under the auspices of a cherished grandfather, who had died young when Josh was only eight. Ever poetic, Josh told me one day with a smile, "You can't do anything about the present, which unfolds before you realize it. The only thing you can change is the past."

Not surprisingly, Josh's marriage exhibited more, not less strain, as he talked more and drank less, since neither he nor his long-suffering, long-enabling (in the codependent sense) wife was easily able to encompass and organize the new and freer contact figures that became possible between them. Divorce threatened, Josh had an affair, she almost had an affair, entered therapy instead, and the two of them at last began to address the issues of contact, particularly sexual contact, that they had avoided or attenuated for so long.

Josh left therapy when he took his new job, and for some time I didn't hear from him, except for one answering machine message in which he informed me that he was celebrating his first anniversary of not drinking ("not," he added with a twinkle in his voice, "that you ever showed the slightest interest in whether I drank myself to death or not!"). Still later, when his mother died, he went back to the bottle, and came back to therapy for a short time. I haven't heard from him since, except for occasional indirect reports of his ongoing battles with other monsters, for the sake of other wanderers now, in the choppy seas of public health care delivery. But great stories live because they are continually reenacted here and now, in the lives of all of us. I've met many more monsters

147

in the years since, figure and ground, in the lives of many people, in and out of therapy. But I still can't hear any reference to Homer, or the Trojan War, or all of Greek mythology for that matter, without thinking of Josh.

THE CASE OF LINDA, OR CIVIL WARS

Josh's life, as he himself conceived it, contained a grounded allusion to ancient myths, and we found it fruitful to "go with" and enter into that metaphor (a kind of experimental therapeutic confluence), by way of understanding the structured personal ground from which Josh's experience took on its particular shape and power. Linda's existence, by contrast, played itself out on a more modern field, metaphorically speaking—the American Civil War, perhaps, or the trenches of World War One. Legally divorced for nearly five years now, Linda's parents remained embroiled in a constant simmer of bickering and character assassination, endlessly rehashing the past, generally by telephone or in the doorways of each other's homes, with occasional boilovers into open public disputes in school lobbies or crowded restaurants. High on the list of topics were childrearing methods in general, Linda's current difficulties in particular, and which parent was the most to blame. An only child who had been adopted in infancy, Linda was the offspring of a union between an American GI and a Vietnamese woman—in other words, she had passed from one war zone to another. Mature and self-possessed beyond her twelve years, Linda regarded me at our first meeting with a sullenness and suspicion which was relieved only by an irrepressible hint of mischief around the eyes. Like Switzerland among the great powers, she had managed her life in a combat zone quite well all these years without any help, thank you, and she had no intention of giving up her independence now. Moreover, she told me quite openly at our first meeting, she didn't like people who told other people what they were thinking and feeling—such as her school counselor, and now me. As for her, her life was going just fine. She was the second most popular girl in seventh grade, she informed me, with parties every weekend and three boyfriends, two of them in upper grades.

148

It was true her grades were not good (in fact, she ws failing three subjects out of five at the time, with a school-tested IQ in the very superior range—"which means the upper one percent," her mother stormed, as she brandished the computer printout under my nose)—but that was only because school didn't interest her. She didn't care if she was failing; all she cared about was her social life. And that, she repeated, was fine, just fine. No problems, end of discussion, it was certainly nice to meet me, she looked forward, frankly, to not seeing me again.

I was both reasured and charmed by this contact initiative, this experimental organization on Linda's part, of the ground of encounter between us. Clearly this was a survivor, and a highly competent one at that. True, I could see perils ahead for her that she might not see, at her age. But what use would a more dependent/confluent organization of contact be to her, in the family field in which she had to operate? Clearly, a less differentiated, less *deflective* stance would be a disaster in that system, as her fused and confused parents illustrated only all too well. If anything, I felt in meeting her steady gaze, this readiness to differentiate, to stand on her own two feet, might be the very thing that would bring her through adolescence relatively unscathed, as long as she could apply the same strategy to her peers and the confluent pressure of the adolescent subculture when she needed it. Denial of distress, which is an aspect or instance of the deflective function, probably becomes a dangerous contact distortion only in conjunction with self-hatred, likewise denied, projected, and then experienced as punishment from the outside. There was nothing of self-punishment or misery in the eyes that met mine now. On the contrary, Linda enjoyed life, even under fairly difficult circumstances—and was enjoying the challenge of managing me right now. It is not a clinical copout to admit that life is a gamble, control illusory; and nowhere is the clincian (or parent) more acutely aware of this than in making judgments about adolescents. I decided to go with my best understanding of Linda's own organization of ground, based in large part on my experience of our encounter in the here and now.

Fine, I told her solemnly, not trying to hide the answering twinkle in my own eyes—there would be absolutely no need for her to like me, now or in the future, in order for us to get our work done. Nor would she likely need to see much of me, since I expected to be working in large part with her parents, trying to get them out of her hair—though I did realize that that was their way of communicating their love, for her and for each other, and certainly I would always be glad to see her, since I enjoyed people who spoke their mind. And certainly I would never presume to know what she was thinking or feeling, though she had to grant that I was an independent person too, and was free to make guesses and have opinions. For instance, I was by no means persuaded that she was so undistressed as she appeared about her failing grades. If nothing else, failing seventh grade would interfere sharply with her social life with her classmates. Furthermore, I wasn't convinced that lack of interest was the only reason for the problem. On the contrary, anybody with her brain power ought to be able to make the honor roll, talk on the telephone, and watch TV all at the same time. If she wasn't, then my guess was that her concentration was being messed with by the constant turmoil with and between her parents. I was interested in what she thought about my guesses, I told her, but we wouldn't really know, in my opinion, unless and until we made the experiment to find out.

"I'm listening," was Linda's reply. Perhaps she liked people who spoke their minds too—which is to say, who exercised the contact function of high differentiation. Unlike her mother, who was looking at me as if I had two heads, or possibly none.

However, I went on, in order for us to perform the experiment, she might have to like me even less, because my advice to her parents was going to be that they stop hassling her, or each other, about anything to do with her schoolwork, and simply make her weekend social life dependent on a certain minimum standard of school performance for the week. She was already receiving a weekly progress card from each teacher—an automatic school structure for children who were failing at midterm. The simplest thing to do, it seemd to me, would be for her just to negotiate an agreement with her parents about what those minimum standards would be, for homework completed, quiz grades, and so forth,—and then any week that the report wasn't up to snuff, she would incur a social restriction, the details of which they could also work out among themselves, there in my office. As for her mother's complaints that she was lying about her assignments, or her quizzes, or her grades—well, we wouldn't have to deal with any of that. Either the teachers would sign the sheet on Friday, confirming that everything was in, or they wouldn't. My advice to her parents would be not to get involved in exceptions, explanations, or excuses, but rather to respect her own independence in managing the work, or not, as she saw fit. Again, I said I'd be interested to know what she thought of such an experiment.

"I think it would work," Linda said evenly. "But not for the reasons you say." Her parents' nagging and fighting didn't bother her, she assured me; I was quite wrong to think it did, or that anything in my power would ever stop them. They had always nagged and fought, and they always would. The experiment would work simply because she cared about her social life. She had no interest in homework, but if it came down to it, she'd rather do it than miss a party. Was it my imagination again, or did the dare behind her eyes say that it never would come down to it anyway— that she could manage her parents all right, and such sanctions would never in fact be enforced?

As it happened, Linda and I were both right on this point. In the weeks that followed, working with her parents on, among other things, the *deflective structure* of the schoolwork contract, neither of them was ever able to impose the contract sanction of making Linda miss one of her treasured weekend parties (or if one did, the other undermined it), as a consequence of a missing signature or check mark on the weekly school sheet. At the same time, her school performance rose significantly—in the absence of any serious negative sanction! From Cs, Ds, and Fs, she finished out the year with Bs, Cs, and one A. Meanwhile, both her parents reported separately a higher incidence of positive interactions and mutually pleasurable activities with Linda—shopping, movies, conversations, and so forth—now that they were not spending all their respective time with her in arguing about the latest school crises.

Not that they had given that up altogether! On the contrary, I would have been surprised and concerned if they had. I had meant it when I said that nagging was an important *contact style*, a communication of connectedness in the system. To give that up would be to remove a central figure of contact without a corresponding reorganization of ground to support the emergence of new strategies, a more flexible range of contact functions and style to meet the system's needs for connection and exchange. Rather, in presenting the idea of the contract, in addition to supporting Linda's autonomy and differentiation in the system, my principal goal was to introduce an experiment in enlarging the contact *repertory* in the family system—in this case, to *add* or support the functions of *deflection* and *disengagement* to a family ground that was structured to favor focusing/concentration and engagement to an overdeveloped degree. Deflection, in that whenever the conflictual figure loomed of strife between parent and child, or parent and parent, at least on the school issue, the ground now included the structure of the contract itself as a possible deflective tool. "We don't have to talk about that, we'll have the answer one way or the other on Friday," was at least prepotently possible in the ground of possible responses to a conflictual contact overture.

In the same way, the institution or structure of therapy itself can serve as a deflection of various contact possibilities: "I/we don't have to deal with that now, I/we can take it up in the therapy hour." As with any other contact function or mode, clearly this can then be used to positive or negative effect, in the sense of enhancing or inhibiting passionate satisfaction in a person's (or system's) life. Certainly we all know people who use the fact and structure of therapy as a deflection of living—to say nothing of all the therapists who are more easily present, more completely engaged in their professional hours than outside them. In the case of Linda's parents, ever on the hairtrigger for a new exchange of salvos, I was hardly worried about their deflecting all of this passion into therapy. Rather, the experiment as I understood it took place in a ground in which all or most of the energy for any *other* passionate living was deflected into this single figure of combat. The *meaning* of the figure, as we have been arguing all through these pages, always has to be sought and understood in the ground. Thus the wider purpose of the experiment here had to do with the constriction in overall contact possibilities in the lives of all the members of the family system, Linda as well as her parents.

This illustrates in turn a crucial difference of conception, if not necessarily of initial approach, between the Gestalt perspective and that of the various "family systems" schools, to this and similar family problems. That is, any approach which is fundamentally *behavioral* (as opposed to the *awareness* approaches, a dichotomization which would locate the Gestalt and psychodynamic schools on the same side of the boundary) will by definition tend to be *solution-oriented.* The work of Minuchin comes to mind (1974; and see also Gurman & Kniskern (1981), for a discussion of differences of emphasis among systemic, structural, and strategic family work), bearing in mind of course, as discussed in earlier chapters, that no behavioral work can ever actually take place without a *reorganization of awareness* and that the best behaviorists, like the best psychodynamicists, cheat liberally, in the theoretical sense—and by our arguments, in a Gestalt direction!

But the problem with symptom- or solution-oriented work, as Freud pointed out long ago, is that the *symptom/problem* itself is the dynamic solution to another, "deeper" problem (is itself a creative adjustment, Goodman would say). Thus the common complaint of beginning clinicians, on first trying out the sort of "behavioral-contract" approach to family problems described here: surprises and pleasure first, at the rapidity with which the presenting symptom is initially dissolved—followed quickly by surprised chagrin at how little the members of the system like the solution, which was not yet supported by changes in *ground, and how busily they may work to undermine the solution* in favor of *status quo ante* (a phenomenon known to the psychodynamic schools as the problem of "secondary gains"). Then follows, on many occasions at least, a rupture or shift in both conception and treatment of the problem, as various system members (those who have not already left treatment) are "spun off" into individual therapy to explore the reasons, in a historical/etiological sense, for their "resistance."

In the Gestalt approach as we have been outlining it here, no such radical gearshift in therapy need take place (which is not to say, of course, that there will be no more breakdowns in treatment). Again, what we are claiming for the Gestalt model, as revised here, is the ability to move between and among different systemic *levels*—intrapsychic, interpersonal, whole-system—in the same language, and to do this whether the initial presentation, the presenting client, is an individual, a couple, or a group. By conceiving presenting (figural) symptoms as a set of contact *strategies*, as well as contact and awareness problems, in a structured ground, the present dynamic meaning of figure can be considered in various grounds (individual, family, and so forth), and these various meanings can be related to each other—again, in the same theoretical language. Thus our experiment is not best understood, in Gestalt, as a trial solution to a problem, or even a trial excursion into a new contact strategy (though it is certainly both of these things as well), but as first and foremost an *exploration of structured ground.* Far from being surprised that a new "solution," a new contact strategy, poses or reveals a new problem, we are primarily interested in the first place in the exploration of these structures of ground which the new "problem," in relation to the old one, lays bare.

In this case, the meaning of the figure of conflict was different, in the dynamic, Lewinian sense (of viewing present behavior as necessarily caused by present dynamics), for each member of the system. For Linda's father, what emerged as some of the chronic strife was deflected/contained into the contract and the therapy hour was primarily *loneliness.* As with nations, endemic warfare both prevented and spared him from getting on with his life. Without the daily harangue from his ex-wife when he came in from work each evening, he confessed ruefully, his answering machine was likely to be bare. If it wasn't his evening to be with Linda for dinner, and he couldn't phone up the house and pass an hour in vigorous competitive blaming, he really didn't know what to do with himself. He found himself tempted to drink, or calling Linda to get a long report on her day (since without having seen her for at least twenty-four hours, he didn't even have any new data to use as ammunition with her mother). Small wonder if Linda was suspicious of any effort to destructure that persistent conflict figure, which might then be reorganized more directly around her! She needed her parents to keep fighting, no matter what the cost in chaotic and distracting ground conditions for her and her schoolwork, if the alternative was a heavier burden for her, meeting the contact needs of a superficially competent but actually dependent, empty father.

As for her mother, she had taken the step, at least, of forming a new relationship with a potential long-term partner, someone whose existence I was not even aware of for a time, so engrossing was the ongoing battle between the divorced spouses. The only trouble was, this new relationship was completely conflict-free— and this was a woman whose whole life had been spent in connections built principally around conflict, as a contact strategy. What on earth would happen to her new romance, she blurted out one day in a panic, if she were to stop fighting with Linda's father, or with Linda—or even to cut down? Two things, I told her, in answer to her rhetorical question. First, she would get a lot closer to her new friend, for better or for worse, or both. And second, if she wanted that relationship to survive the shift, she'd better keep working on some new strategies for closeness, to support and supplement the single ground structure of prepotent conflict she had relied on for so long.

Over the next couple of years Linda's family underwent a steady series of significant changes, some clearly positive, others not so clear. Linda continued to make mostly Cs in school, with few honor grades, much to the continuing distress of her mother. Her mother eventually married her new friend and had a baby—something which might be expected to discombobulate any adolescent half-sibling, especially an adopted one, but which didn't appear to faze Linda. She took the baby in stride, pronounced him adorable, but gave her parents to understand in no uncertain terms that she was quite busy with her own life in high school now, thank you, and couldn't be expected to raise him. Linda's father also formed a new relationship, broke it off, went into a deep depression, and ultimately sought help from a psychiatrist who relied heavily on medication. In other words, they got on with their lives, for well and ill. Somewhere along the way they went back to their divorce lawyer (they had both used the same one, unofficially) to hammer out a regular arrangement of residence and visitation schedules for Linda (who honored this piece of paper more in the breach than in the observance), because they were "tired of always fighting about the schedule."

As for Linda, when I last saw her she paid me the high compliment of saying I might have helped her mother "a little." She also took pains to point out, in memory of our first standoff, that in four years she had missed plenty of homework assignments, but never yet failed a course or missed a party. So did the contract work, or didn't it, I wanted to know? Hard to say, was Linda's reply. Certainly it had helped her parents, and we might even say it had helped her get them off her back. As for helping her directly—and here the twinkle in Linda's eye again spoke volumes, or at any rate seduced me into feeling it spoke volumes—how could it possibly do that, when she never had a problem in the first place?

VII

The Structure of Ground Continued: Two Systems Cases

THE UNRESISTANT SYSTEM

IN THE previous chapter we took a long and then a shorter look at two "clinical" cases, one "individual" and one "family," with the idea of examining what new possibilities of understanding and intervention for change are opened up or cast in a different light by all the theoretical discussion that had gone before. In particular we were interested in the questions of how consideration of structured features of ground, enduring patterns of behavior over time (which are variously called behavioral sets, defense mechanisms, or personality dynamics by other theoretical models) shape and yield the emerging figure, and how attention to these ground structures in the process of Gestalt analysis changes and enlarges our understanding of figure formation and the contact process.

Now before a final summing up of all these arguments, we will be considering two more cases, again one longer and one shorter, this time from the "organizational" or "systems" domain (a boundary which has already been breached by the "family" case above, and which in any case should be illusory, by our argument and by Goodman's). In these cases we will continue to have in mind all the questions considered in the previous chapter, plus the additional claim (from Chapter V, and discussed again in the "family" case) that we are at last working toward a theoretical model that would support us to talk about problems at the intra- and interpersonal levels in the same language—and bearing in mind as we go along that if these two levels have been historically difficult to combine in psychological models, it is Goodman first and foremost who teaches us to expect that such an integration should be both fruitful and possible.

"BBS" was and is a private, progressive, suburban elementary school, religously affiliated, for whom I had provided some clinical consulting services in the past. While the staff and students were quite heterogeneous by religion and ethnicity, the parent church organization provided a majority of the Board and managed to set the overall policy and tone, which were generally educationally and socially liberal: no letter grades, teachers and children on a first-name basis, active recruiting and funding of minority students, much attention to group process and political issues, and so forth. If in some ways BBS was an island in time, in the more conservative period when the present consultation took place, it was on the whole a happy island: bright, relaxed faces, a reasonably orderly and productive environment, and a long record of patient and fruitful support of youngsters the traditional schools didn't seem able to reach. Clearly the institution was a success, in anybody's terms, in all the kinds of problems which were amenable to what we may call the *dominant contact style* of the organization—which is to say, a highly understanding, supportive, person-to-person style or approach; what we might call, using our traditional Gestalt language, a highly "confluent" style, with (in our revised terms here) a corresponding weakness at the opposite pole, of differentiation/resistance itself. Not surprisingly, it was that opposite pole, or the relative absence of it as a contact resource in the ground of the organization, that was giving them trouble now.

Nor was I surprised that they called me. When in doubt, BBS always went with someone they already knew, someone reliably "like us,"—a kind of xenophobia in staffing matters that was a curious polar counterpart to their open embrace of all classes, all backgrounds among the students themselves. Never mind that the work I had done for them in the past had had to do with the clinical evaluation of five-year-olds, applicant children of established BBS families who were seen as possibly inappropriate for the stimulating and loosely structured program of the school. I had dealt somehow with those families without losing them for the school; therefore, I must be someone who could "handle conflict" and "resolve differences," yet without going over to the "others"—i.e., those people or forces in the outside world that were perceived as dehumanizing, bureaucratic, or downright politically incorrect. Now that the Headmaster was embroiled in a simmering conflict that threatened to boil over and involve the whole faculty, something clearly had to be done. To call in a consultant at all, I gathered (and could well imagine, from my previous contacts with the school), felt like a defeat of sorts, for the Head especially—a breakdown in some sense of their cherished belief that all problems, all conflicts, could be resolved by dint of renewed dedication to the proposition that we are fundamentally one, that apparent differences are illusory, and that they disappear when we meditate together on all the things that unite us. From our Gestalt perspective, clearly this is confluence with a vengeance, and at the same time a powerful ideology, and a powerful, if partial, truth. Still, if they had to have a "professional," with all the structures and overtones that the word implied, then better the devil they knew!

Not that the phone call came from the Headmaster. On the contrary, it was the Chairman of the Board who called, although she hastened to assure me that the Head was "aware" of her intention and "not opposed" to the idea. This calls to mind the old dictum from process consulting, which derives in turn from psychoanalytic transference theory, that the circumstances of the initial contact with the consultant, the approach, the contracting, the limits or absence thereof, recapitulate the process problem of the organization itself. Once again, as was discussed in Chapter I, we are dealing here with an insight from psychodynamic theory, which is itself best explained by the concepts of the Gestalt awareness model. Clearly, it requires little if any translation to turn the above proposition, about conditions of entry of the consultant into the organizational field, into our Gestalt language—and particularly if we include our expanded terminology of structured features of ground, as prepotent or limiting contact conditions, as developed here. In this case, what we may call the "contact themes" of unclear role boundaries, avoidance of sharp differentiation, and the recurrent condition of a weak yes covering an unstated no (an unenergized confluence, in terms of contact functions, which is actually undermined or limited by the absence of clear *differentiation/resistance*, in the contact repertory), were all characteristic themes and styles in the life of the organization in general, as would only become increasingly clear as the consultation went on.

Since we are conceiving these themes as *ground structures* over time, and not just momentary contact figures (or "resistances" to momentary contact figures), it follows necessarily that we would expect to see that style in most if not all specific figures of encounter, and likewise that we should expect to be able to "read the ground" of the organization, at least hypothetically/diagnostically (and a diagnosis is always a hypothesis, and a hypothesis about *ground*), from a particular figure or series of figures of the moment. In the familiar Gestalt percept, the whole determines the parts, at least as much as the other way around: this is what the Gestalt awareness model is all about. Put in our language here, this is equivalent to saying the *ground determines the figure* (as well as the other way around). But if so, then any figure, any contact moment, properly understood, "contains" the ground as well by implication—in the sense that a different ground would yield a different figure, under the same "external" conditions.

More concretely, the presenting problem in this case had to do with two teachers in the school, both widely perceived as dysfunctional, and both generally seen as "dragging the institution down." Not only were their own teams overburdened with compensating for their dysfunction, but enrollment was actually beginning to fall off in those two particular grades—clearly a problem that once started, could only spread, as the undersized classes passed on up through the grade levels. This had been worsening for at least two years now, and still the Head refused to do anything definite about it. My job, as the Board Chair put it, was to talk to the Head, persuade him as I had persuaded those unhappy parents some time ago that these two teachers were simply inappropriate to their placements, and that he would be doing everybody a favor to "bite the bullet" and send them on their way. In other words, if the Head was not doing his job right (at least in the perception of some), then rather than confronting him directly (a figure of highly *differentiated* or *resistant contact*, in our language), the Chair would simply take that part of the problem over. Then, since she couldn't do it either, she was turning it over to me! This, of course, is a sequence of moves, or overtures at least, familiar to anyone who has worked much with organizational problems—including family problems, or clinical work with children ("You'll have to knock some sense into him, Doctor—I can't do a thing with him!").

The Head, when I spoke with him, was generally in agreement with everything the Chairman had told me, in the best spirit of progressive self-criticism. Yes, it was true that these two teachers had serious problems, one rather more than the other. And yes, it was true that he himself would find it very difficult, if not impossible, to fire anyone for mere dysfunction, when that person was still trying his best to do the job. Weren't we all a family here, a spiritual family even? (It began to come back to me at this point that it was the teachers, not the Head, who had asked my help in keeping those particular children out of the school. Left to himself, the Head would have accepted them.) Certainly he was aware of the problems, and even of the wider rumblings of discontent; that was why he was devoting so much time to those two teachers, meeting with them, advising them, taking over their classrooms at times, even insisting that they seek psychotherapy (this last was offered, apparently, as a gesture of conciliation to me). However (and here his tone changed somewhat as he drew on his own contact resources for differentiation and resistance), each human being was uniquely valuable. It was not for him as Head Teacher (the role he conceived for himself) to judge that this or that person was inappropriate for membership in our community. If the community seemed to suffer, momentarily, by carrying two weaker members, then that was something the community should be able to accept. In any case (and now at last came something even more steely, under the soft-spoken manner), that was how he saw it: if the Board didn't like it, they certainly knew what they could do about it.

But did they? It seemed to me quite unlikely that they did, any more than the Head knew what to do with these two teachers, for all his sincere invocation of values issues. By way of opening the exploration of ground, I asked the Head how he himself was evaluated, and how his performance judgment was arrived at by the Board, what the procedures were for feedback, contracting, job description, and so forth. Needless to say, there were none. Sometime around the end of each year, if he remembered to think about it, he simply wrote a one-line contract memo to himself, signed it, and put it in the Chairman's box. What became of it from there, he had no idea. Frankly, it had never occurred to him to wonder. Certainly if it came under official Board discussion at any time he would know about it, since he attended all Board meetings, and all meetings of the Executive Committee. As for unofficial discussion, it was hard to imagine any conversation in the community that was not instantly public property, albeit sometimes in distorted versions.

When later I put the same question to the teachers, I received much the same answer. Despite occasional promises by the Head to "tighten up on procedures," there were no definite contracting dates, no written job descriptions, no performance reviews, regular or irregular. Whereas in the past this latitude was associated with freedom and creativity on the job, now many of the teachers were clear and expressive about the negative aspects of such extreme informality. In the present crisis, for instance, without clear and public support from above, it was very difficult for them even to try to help the team members that were hurting, since in order to broach the subject they would have to take up the position of judges of their colleagues' inferior performance. As for themselves, some of them volunteered that they were coming to understand the occasional complaints of older students, who said they "didn't know where they stood" without tests and letter grades. In the case of a job well done, these teachers felt the lack of clear praise; and even in other cases, they could imagine that if individual professional development tasks were outlined in an official performance review, this could serve as a basis for requesting a training grant from the Board. From time to time, they had asked the Head to initiate such procedures, but he never followed through. The problem must be, many teachers agreed, a "personal hangup" of the Head's. Some suggested psychotherapy (again!); others, assertiveness training. Nobody suggested changing Heads; all parties agreed, apparently, that in most respects he was doing a fine job. Everyone professed to be fond of him, and to respect him as a Head Teacher and curriculum leader. It was only in this one area that he needed retooling. No one suggested that it might be difficult for anybody, hangup or no hangup, to take an assertive/judgmental action (in our language, form a figure of highly *differentiated contact*) that ran so strongly counter to the tenor and texture (again, in our language, the structured ground) of life in general at the school.

With this in mind, and supposing that the teachers' own unexplored ambivalence might well have played a part in blocking the very actions they wanted and needed, I judged that the simplest and most productive intervention at this level of the problem might be to educate the teachers (that is, to attempt a direct change in the ground of their assumptions) about possible structures of evaluation processes, and their various possible professional, emotional, and even moral consequences. Evaluation, after all, is an inherently adversarial process—and adversarial processes were difficult or impossible to initiate or sustain, as contact figures, out of the structured ground of life in this organization as it now stood. Self-evaluation, however—even self-criticism—was a familiar and legitimate potential figure (ground structure) in the religious and political tradition of the school. Likewise, a peer counseling model was a comfortable and nonthreatening prepotent figure in the tradition, and team-teaching too was already available as a preexisting structure. From all of this it was simple to assemble an elementary team-based evaluation structure, based on self-evaluation in peer pairs and then reviewed in the group. All of that could be performed and recorded before the Head was even directly involved; and at the same time, once that much had been done, it would be nearly impossible for the Head to decline to come in on it. He was already meeting regularly with the various teams, who would need only to enter their evaluation reports onto the agenda. Then too, I hoped that a process based on self-evaluation and ratified and backed by the group would serve to allay at least some of everybody's moral and emotional qualms about judging and being judged (which is to say, again, about a kind of bounded or differentiated contact which was relatively absent from the dominant contact style of the organization). As for the problem teachers, such a process might serve as a base, at least, for a more open discussion among the team of just where the problem lay, and what might be done about them (and here again, I was trying to resist, with the "dysfunctional" teachers as with the partly "dysfunctional" Head, buying into the prevailing assumption that all these problems were purely intrapersonal, and not more broadly systemic in the team or in the school in general).

In all of this, what I was doing, in helping the teaching teams develop evaluation processes, was not necessarily different from what another consultant, working from another theoretical frame of reference, might have done with the same problem. Any systems consultant, at least, would certainly have shared my resistance to seeing the problem as purely an intrapsychic issue for the Head, to be resolved by a personnel change at that level. On the other hand, a "pure systems" analyst, realizing how pervasive the avoidance of clear evaluation processes was throughout the organization, might be tempted to overlook or downplay the very real personal and philosophical problems the Head had, with figures of judgment, separation, rejection. It is the particualr capacity of the Gestalt model, and particularly as articulated here, to address both these levels of the problem—the systemic and the personal—and in the same language. More than this, the analysis of contact processes of the organization—and particularly the inclusion of analysis of ground structures, as well as figure formation—sheds light on where the problem at hand, and the wider dominant contact style of the system itself, fit into basic emotional and value predispositions about how contact can and should occur in the life of the organization—predispositions which are themselves enduring and figure-formative structures of ground, which favor certain kinds of figure and disfavor others in an ongoing way. This in turn enables the consultant to speak to the client in his own language, to support and value the *dominant contact style of the organization in relation to the goals and values of that system*, which are again the predisposing, structured ground conditions for the persistent formation of figures of a certain kind, and not others. This supports the possibility—again, one intuited by Freud, but perhaps best explained by an organizational Gestalt model—of understanding the "symptom" not just as a problem but as a *solution misapplied*, which is to say, an awareness disturbance in the field (and recall Goodman's formulation, that neurosis is creative adjustment on the basis of incomplete or blocked awareness; see for example Perls et al., 1951, p. 271).

The organization of experience (which is after all the particular subject matter of Gestalt psychology, of which by all our arguments here the Gestalt psychotherapeutic or consulting model is a part) must have, like all organized processes, some optimal point of "cohesiveness," either more or less than which yields some falling away from "best outcomes," which is to say from satisfaction. Too chaotic a ground, and figures will be formed which are not in keeping with basic goals and values of the system, which may themselves be poorly formulated, not available for clear, strong figure formation (and thus not available as well-organized ground for other strong figures). Organizations, or individuals, with this kind of ground problem have a scattered, chaotic quality, with some parts contradicting others, anomalous impulses and actions, and little ability to mobilize the whole system energetically to move in the direction of any clear goal. Some parts or subsystems may be sluggish; others may be frenetic, without an overall organizing sense of *self* (in the case of an individual) or of "somebody in charge" (in the case of an organization). Thus we speak, in the individual case, of "self" or "character disorders," meaning disorder in the ground in this sense (as opposed to the "psychoses," by which we mean the formation of figures with no understandable relation to ground, or a ground which cannot be consensually or interpersonally influenced). At the same time, it is not difficult to think of organizational examples of the same thing, sometimes on a very large scale: both the Democratic Party and the Reagan White House, for example, come readily to mind. In all such cases, the likely intervention for change will be in the area known as "core mission" work—a phrase which is obviously not hard to translate into our terminology of structured ground (see for example discussion in Argyris & Schon, 1978). Clinically, as we have argued at various points through these chapters, the same disorder may best be addressed by the ongoing experiment of having to *use* the disordered self in a "real encounter" in the field—which is to say, in a close and careful process of *relationally* based therapy.

On the other hand, as in the case of BBS, it may be that the ground of the system is *too* tightly organized, too rigidly "fixated," in Goodman's term (Perls et al., 1951, p. 403), to permit the free and flexible relationship between basic ground structures (goals and values) and the changing conditions of the momentary situation—a relationship which is the very definition of figure formation and destruction itself. To use the richly suggestive phrase, there is no "play" in the system—in the senses both of looseness or openness of fit, and also of playfulness, lightness of touch. Certain kinds of figures (in our language, certain contact functions, traditionally called "resistances") are ruled out, or at least regarded with a grim, unplayful eye. Ironically, as we have seen in this case, this rigidity of ground can come to surround or underlie even figures of openness or confluence itself.

In these cases, our model would suggest, the intervention should support a process of destructuring of rigid or simplistic ground features, so that a richer and more complex structure, one that permits organization of more of the field (greater awareness) in terms of the felt goals, can take their place. In other words, a contact or organization of the self/system in the field that yields more satisfying outcomes, in the system's own terms (and recall here the arguments of Chapter V, that the relevant criteria of health and dysfunction are not best drawn from an arbitrary list of "good" and "bad" process habits or "resistances," but from the person or system's own goals and outcomes). I had already tried to begin this process at BBS by supporting the formation of the new team evaluation procedures—both to demystify or "detoxify" the evaluative process itself as a missing function in organizational life, and to violate (or destructure) certain "ground rules," of not asserting role boundaries or formal processes, all in hopes of sending out ripples, or perhaps tremors, through the organized ground of the school community.

Once this structure was in place, and began to get a good press around the school community, I decided to take the plunge and try the same thing at the other end (speaking in terms of the organizational hierarchy which was avoided or denied in the school). The Head, after all, hierarchically speaking, was an employee of the Board. How can you expect, I asked the Chairman, that the Head will be able to do something with his employees that you yourselves are unable or afraid to do with yours? Either the Board must institute a regular evaluation process with the Head, along the not-too-threatening lines of the emerging teacher-evaluation model, or else it must give up expecting the Head to act in a role-bounded way with problem personnel. Such a process, I argued (now with teacher support), far from undermining the Head, would actually support him in all his functioning. Moreover, since it was well-known that the community as a whole was quite satisfied, in the main, with the Head's performance, now was the time to institute these processes, which might serve the school well in the event of some crisis in the future.

This time the seismic shocks were much greater. The Head threatened resignation; it was the teachers, in the end, who talked him out of it, person-to-person, promising him that the school would not "turn into General Motors" with the institution of certain formal, role-defined structures and processes. On the contrary, they argued, they themselves were *freed up*, personally and professionally, by the very evaluative processes he was viewing as inherently dehumanizing and restrictive. This last had been my argument, with teachers and Head alike, from the first; and it was here that the Gestalt perspective, and particularly our view here of the importance of understanding *organized ground*, were of crucial support, and added a dimension that other consulting models might have neglected. For in the case of a system with a strong sense of core mission, and in some ways an overorganized ground, the model and perspective we are developing here suggest strongly that it is useless to work *against* the dominant contact style of the organization—because that dominant style, which might otherwise be conceived as a "resistance to contact," is actually structurally related to the central values and goals in the organized ground of the system itself. A consultant (which is to say a "figure" of encounter, or potential encounter) who cannot "get inside" that understanding, that ground, will likely be extruded from the organized field—much like the kinds of potential figures which are already being ruled out, and whose absence has already been defined as the very problem the consultant is trying to address.

Rather, the consultant (or the psychotherapist, in the clinical case) has to appreciate how the dominant contact style of the system grows out of and contributes to the system's own goals and values, and then find ways of bringing into awareness how the absence of the corresponding functional pole (in this case, differentiation or resistance itself) is actually undermining those goals and that dominant, *chosen* style—and how the judicious development of that missing polar function can be used to *support* and energize that valued style, and the achievement of those chosen goals. This proposition, after all, is the very essence of the perspective articulated in Chapter V: namely, that any function, any contact mode, will become rigid, deenergized, and ultimately dysfunctional in the absence of *support from its own polar counterpart*—and that this is necessarily, theoretically true by the terms of the Gestalt model as we have articulated it here, giving equal emphasis in contact analysis to figure formation/destruction, and structured ground. Far from needing to give up or get over the "resistance" of "confluence," which after all was crucially embedded in the value system and world view of the organization, what BBS as a system needed to learn was how to *use resistance*, as an essential contact function, in the service of their wider confluent goals.

With this in mind, and drawing again on another established structure of the parent church organization, I organized (with the Chairman) a "meeting for concern," a kind of discussion session or symposium around a particular ethical topic—in this case, termination or firing, whether of staff or students, from the school community. Here the overall, destructuring goal was to *differentiate* notion of role from the notion of personhood, and to discriminate, in a moral sense, between evaluation of performance and judgment of intrinsic personal worth. As with the other interventions, after a shaky start the miniconference went swimmingly, to all appearances, and was pronounced a success. Even the Head volunteered that he was considering for the first time the notion that you don't necessarily "support" a person's value and development by keeping him on in an inappropriate job placement.

At this point, the consultation seemed to be nearing an end on an apparently successful note, with many obvious and pervasive changes in the general life of the school. The Board had survived a first evaluation of the Head; teaching teams were meeting and filing written self- and peer-evaluations; even students were participating in evaluation conferences, again based on a self-evaluation and discussion model. And yet the original problem hadn't changed! Two teachers were still in great distress and widely perceived as not up to the job—and still the Head declined to take steps, which is to say, to make more resistant contact with them than he had been able to do so far. Privately, he confessed to me, his deepest hope was that these problems would "go away by themselves"—i.e., that the teachers in question would resign.

Nothing I had done had made him more able to address the problem himself, in any nonconfluent way.

One teacher did just that, under the pressure, support, or awareness clarification of the self- and team-evaluation procedures, which led her to the conclusion that far from being overwhelmed by unmanageable personal issues, she was simply in the wrong line of work, or at least the wrong corner of the line. The other teacher, more severely dysfunctional, was recontracted as usual (after many heart-to-heart talks with the Head). Summer came; the Head made plans to depart as scheduled on a long-planned semester's sabbatical out of the country. One of the faculty was appointed Acting Head for the semester, and the new year began. At this point—and I was watching the process from a somewhat greater distance now—the faculty rose up in support of the Acting Head, who was able (after a transatlantic courtesy call to the Head) to assert the long-missing boundary. The teacher in question resigned under pressure, and the whole community—including no doubt the Head, and likely the teacher herself—breathed an enormous sigh of relief. Since the school was still unable to make a clear boundary with me, I took it on myself to declare the contract closed, and the consultation over. To be consistent, I insisted on an evaluation form for the consult itself, but most of the process took place in my own mind.

Much later, questions persisted. Clearly, the community as a whole—teachers, Board, even students—had been ready to embrace the new process structures and new functional contact possibilities offered in the consultation, particularly when they were couched in the *ground language* of the organization's own goals and values. Why then had the Head, "at" whom the consult was originally aimed, been so little influenced by the whole process? Had I, in my eagerness to be more than "just a clinician," to show that I could view things in a systemic perspective, been blind to real intrapsychic issues which I might have addressed more directly? The Head was forever recommending psychotherapy to others; was this because he wanted and needed it for himself? When the Head returned from his sabbatical (to a school just buzzing with evaluative processes all over the place, with the enthusiasm of converts), he announced that he would be leaving for good at the end of that year, to return to teaching. Had I pushed him out—and if so, was that a good thing or a bad thing, for the school?

The next Head, chosen no doubt in a sort of group reaction formation, proved to be a disaster of the opposite extreme— precisely because he was unable to understand and appreciate the kind of ground structures of core value and mission that we have been analyzing here. Was it grandiose to wonder if this fiasco, and the ensuing two years of chaos in the school, were in part my fault? And if so, what might I have done differently to support a more fluid, more cohesive integration of the expanded contact reper- toire of the organization, so as to avoid this subsequent jerkiness of process (itself symptomatic of a newly *dis*organized ground, as discussed above)? If only I had stayed on, whispers the voice of grandiosity, letting the contract elide into a regular, ongoing con- sultancy without anybody's much noticing, in the characteristically diffuse, role-boundless way of the school's life. Then I would have been there to prevent their next mistake! And thus the consul- tant succumbs, in fantasy at least, to the process "bug" of the system itself—in this case, the boundless, confluent stance of be- ing all things to all people, and taking care of (and thereby infan- tilizing) the whole world forever.

These are imponderables, and represent, among other things, the characteristic fantasies and feelings of termination and withdrawal in the contact cycle—the same feelings and regrets that were operating to make BBS as a whole, and the Head in particular, try repeatedly to skip over or avoid this phase of contact, which is loss itself. Without my help (and perhaps even a little bit because of it, at the earlier stage of this consultation), BBS recovered from its next period of crisis, reorganized in a more coherent way, and is to all appearances a thriving institution today. Contact, which is to say investment, does involve loss and regret, as well as poten- tial satisfaction, achievement, and pride. Children, clients, and other objects of nurturance do grow up and make it, or not, on their own: let every consultant, therapist, teacher, or parent ig- nore this at his or her own peril!

A FINAL CASE: "GESTALT" RECONSIDERED

And now, again for balance, let us take a look at a much briefer case, in the life of a more transient organization, with different, nearly opposite contact problems, in the example below: contact disturbances in a Gestalt training group.

The criteria of health or dysfunction, systemically or individually, as we have argued all through these chapters (and especially in Chapter V), must be sought not in some preordained list of "resistances," which may by our model be only polar halves of necessary contact functions, but rather in the goals and needs of the organized system itself, and in the question of whether the available contact functions do or do not lead to satisfaction of those needs, in the system's own terms. Put more simply, an organization (or person) needs to have at its disposal those functional contact possibilities that will get it where it wants to go. For my client Josh, under the severely retroflective, unexpressive contact style he had developed (for good reason, originally) over thirty-odd years, it was almost unimaginable that he would be able to give up or even moderate his drinking—or that his life would be much better if he did. For those things to happen, he first had to enlarge his contact repertory—which meant, prior even to that, *imagining* and experiencing the possibility and validity of any other approach to the world, than his own constricted, self-punitive style. Likewise for Linda's family, the contact-supportive function of deflection (originally in the guise of a simple behavioral contract) had to be added "to the pot," in order for destructuring and growth to take place. And again in the case of the progressive school: the problem as conceived here was that existing ground structures, predilections for certain behavioral figures and not others, meant a relative failure to reach the organization's own goals in a fully energized and satisfying way.

At least two of these cases, at their various levels, involve in one way or another a failure of differentiated, bounded, or resistant contact, in our terms here—and not only an excess of "a resistance to contact," as in the traditional language. (The third case, of Linda and her family, involved reliance on an apparently "resistant" or conflictual contact style in the service of covering or distancing other feelings, other needs.) The intervention chosen, in both the individual and organizational cases, was one of supporting the client to experiment with and experience a more *resistant contact*, while managing to avoid or else bearing together the various feared catastrophic consequences. But any polar contact function, we have argued, can be dysfunctional if it is hypertrophied in relation to its complementary function or functions, and if this dominant, inflexible style gets in the way of satisfying figure resolution, because of structured distortions in ground. The following case was very nearly the reverse of those two—a system which, like Linda's family though for quite different reasons, could only permit "contact" at all, in the everyday sense of meetings between people, by assertion of resistance, differentiation, and an insistent rigidity at the boundary.

The system in question was a training group in its final year of a three-year, twelve-week post-graduate training course in Gestalt methodology, at a training institute in a large French city. The training format was one in which trainer/therapists were commonly imported for the week-long sessions, four times a year—often from the other side of the Atlantic, where Gestalt methods were considered to be the most advanced. This structure meant that while the training group came to have a long history together, as such programs go, the therapist/teachers, in both the daytime didactic sessions and the evening therapy groups, were new to the system, and thus not a part of the shared history and norms of the group, which is to say the developing features of shared structured ground.

I had been particularly interested to see, my first time out, what a French-speaking professional group would make of Gestalt theory and methods, and how they would compare as students to their American counterparts. All during the first morning and afternoon, I was not disappointed. The class was bright, engaged, intellectually somewhat combative in the French manner, very much interested in theoretical questions for their own sake (often giving them a political/ideological spin, also a characteristically French habit of thought). On a practical level, the group was mature and efficient, as I had occasion to observe that first morning session. As it happened, the group opened with some dispute with their director of training about contract terms. Immediately the class became a productive work group, smoothly allocating roles and functions, one acting as spokesperson, another taking notes, others taking up various supporting roles, seriously but without undue solemnity. In short, all the signs of a good working group, purposeful, differentiated, and full of good-humored camaraderie. Even the confrontation itself, while intense, was without rancor, and was resolved satisfactorily with good closure and a smooth passage to other work well before the morning coffee break.

Then came the evening, and the first therapy session. Silence, and more silence. Gone was all the lively spontaneity, the atmosphere of lighthearted confrontation, the joking affectionate banter of a group that had been through the wars together across some ten weeks of training. Gone too was the energy for work and serious purpose. In their place as a roomful of dour, fatigued faces—and more silence. Where had the lively learning group of the morning gone? What was the change in ground that had so radically altered the presenting figure? As the evening wore on, the answers slowly, painfully emerged.

Someone was irritated, briefly, with someone else: a weak attempt was made to engage in some discussion. "C'est ta propre merde," came the immediate reply, and several onlookers agreed, "That's your own shit." End of discussion. Someone else felt distress, of some kind, at being left out of a subgroup plan for some free-time activity. "That's your own fault, you exclude yourself," was the curt response. Then more silence. No further expression of feeling, no healthy defensiveness beyond that one remark, no feeling around for a series of transactions, an incremental mutual accumulation of injuries, disappointments, dislikes over time. And yet the group had nothing but time!—time past, and time ahead, stretching endlessly through the week to come. Between my jet-lag and the soporific quality of the process, I began to wonder seriously how I was going to make it through the week—a private figure of concern that had to stand in some way, as always, for the whole group. Yet no private figures became public, no shared articulation, which *is the group itself*, took place. Why was this? Was there some trauma, some signal group event in their history together, of which I was unaware? But if so, then why the highly energized, shared work process of the morning? As long as I could keep my eyes open, I waited, to get more feel for the ground.

And so it went. Every time a serious interpersonal or group issue was raised, it was immediately thrown back on the person raising it, with the interpretive question of why that person was bent on avoiding his/her responsibility for creating his or her own life, in the given situation. Not surprisingly, such issues were seldom raised, and then not with much force or passion. If any member went so far as to ask for something, he or she was "playing helpless," trying to "manipulate the group" (and note the etymology of the word, which means to work "hands on"—the very thing they couldn't do!). If a reproach was made, that too was "avoiding responsibility" (except for the reproach of avoiding responsibility itself, which was not taken as an instance of avoiding responsibility . . .) Responsibility for oneself, of course, never for anyone else as well as oneself, or for a relationship, or for the group as a whole. If an explanation was nevertheless offered in response, however tentatively, then that person was guilty of "avoiding confrontation," or else "avoiding contact," since the two terms were taken as equivalent.

In other words, here we had again a system in which the dominant contact mode or function was retroflective or isolative—only this time in combination with a highly bounded contact style, rather than a confluent one, as in the case of Josh. The structure of group ground (which interacts with but is quite a different animal from structured features of individual, personal ground) was such that figures of self-support and differentiation alone were allowed to emerge somewhat freely, while those of caring, nurturant support, or even exploration of others or of the group as a whole were actively discouraged, through ridicule, "clinical" labeling, or other attack. Questions, it goes without saying, were officially taboo (because asking a question, as for example about what someone meant, or how he or she felt, is "not Gestalt"). Under the given contact circumstances, then, small wonder if hardly any contact at all (even belligerent contact) which *crossed an interpersonal boundary* was allowed, and that which was, was fleeting and unsustained. In our terminology, the ground structures to support such figures simply were not there.

In short, and not to put too fine a point on it, what I was seeing was a system which had been "Gestalt-traumatized," to the point where any figure which did not seem to conform to some caricatured notion of late-Perlsian autonomy was taken to represent a cowardly and dangerous collapse to immature dependency. "Gestalt," locally defined, meant a rigid retroflective self-sufficiency, or counterdependence, of the type discussed at length in Chapter II and taken up again in subsequent chapters. But in all fairness to Perls, he was not particularly interested in group process issues, and certainly never authorized, in the name of "Gestalt," a kind of *group* norm which would ape or travesty certain aspects of his own *individual* therapeutic style. In therapeutic terms, in place of the Gestalt process model offered by Zinker

(1977) and others, whereby the group process and evolving structure itself become the material for group experiment and analysis, in this case the group had moved from a restricted ground which permitted only certain resistant figures, to almost no process at all, beyond the symptom itself, of inability to sustain any figures of contact whatever, combative/autonomous or otherwise.

And yet—and yet—what were those tiny hand signals that passed from time to time from one group member to another, exchanges of meaningful glances, stifled signs of private jokes and shared understandings, that made the group vaguely reminiscent of teaching, say, fifth grade? Was I the enforcer here, and were these people actually cheating on the system they themselves were supposedly endorsing (always remembering, with Goodman, that the universal and irrepressible capacity to subvert a rigid system is ever one of the most saving human graces)? Yes, they confessed with rueful smiles when confronted, they were "cheating the system." And why not give those same gestures openly, verbally, in the group? Because—what else—that "wouldn't be Gestalt."

All this I let go with a wry comment. A stronger "pure awareness" intervention "this-is-what-we're-allowed-and-this-is-our-existence," might well have yielded something new—an intensification, at least, of the paralysis, perhaps with an accompanying outcry or protest. However, once again I wondered how fresh this would be for the group. After all, they were well of aware of the constriction of their predicament, and the limitations on permissible process within the group, in terms of the kinds of figures that could be offered. What they perhaps knew less well was how impoverished even those "resistant" figures themselves had become (in a striking complementary reversal to the school discussed above, where it was the *absence* of fully-formed "resistant" figures that was undercutting or impoverishing the desired confluent contact). If I read them right, they were spoiling at this point for nothing so much as a good fight!—in place of the feeble and episodic spats that were all that could develop under given ground conditions.

The next time an emotionally charged difference emerged, I intervened to stop the process, with the demand/proposal, as an investigative experiment, that before proceeding any further with the fight itself, we first examine the ground conditions of interpersonal support, which by our Gestalt model should underlie the emerging social figure, and support it (or not) through a fully energized cycle to a satisfying conclusion. Since the group had no idea what I was talking about (or rather, no idea that they could readily integrate into their understanding of "Gestalt group"), this meant stopping for a minisymposium on the nature of interpersonal support, and the possible roles it might usefully break down into. At this point the group's astonishment at this "ungestalt" behavior was perhaps matched only by their relief at getting a twenty-minute furlough from "group." After all, as I already knew, "work group" or "seminar" was a ground they knew well how to be in, how to "be themselves" and obtain satisfaction. What they didn't know—couldn't know, by the rigidly autonomous version of Gestalt they had absorbed or synthesized—was how to map any of that ground onto or around the fixed structural features they understood as "Gestalt group" (and here culture comes into play, since autonomy itself is if anything an even more rigid ground value in French culture than in American, and somewhat less mitigated by polar values and myths that support community).

Very quickly four or five major roles began to fall out, which the group agreed were either indispensable or at least potentially central to satisfying conflict: (1) the "copain" or buddy—that sympathetic and largely uncritical friend, who always can see things from your *emotional* point of view, and at times may even speak for the feelings you are overlooking; (2) the more "resistant" friend, yet still a friend—who sees what you don't see in the situation, yet still affirms or empathizes with you and your experience; (3) the "other"—your adversary, perhaps, or some ally of your adversary, a benchmark of difference who can be counted on to see things entirely differently (if this one agrees with you for once, you can be sure you're right! Likewise, if your *adversary's* other, who may also be one of your "soft supports," as they put it, agrees with *him*, then you know you're wrong, in the sense of overlooking something crucial—and thus the structure of your adversary's support system becomes important and useful for you as well, and for you to know and understand); (4) the "translator"—the one who can understand what you are saying (or not saying) and put it in terms your adversary can hear, or vice versa. And so on, with refinements in the two general categories, of *sameness and difference* (confluence and differentiation) that underlie all contact, by the terms of our model. These refinements will be given (and here we are leaving the group's phenomenological language, in favor of our terminology of contact functions) by the goals of the particular system at hand, in relation to the *dominant contact style* discussed above. Thus the confluent school needed "resistant" role support as a contact resource, whether in one person (the consultant, for example), or—ideally—spread among many or all the system's members, at various times, as a potential contact figure. And likewise here, where something like the converse was the case. This in turn yields a possible reformulation (though hardly a new conception, in other process models) of the terms of the consultant role, or for that matter the therapist: namely, first the provision, then the teaching/enabling, and finally the emerging support of those *missing contact functions*, which must be available in the structured ground, for satisfying outcomes (which is to say, figure formation and figure destruction) in the system's own terms.

Here too we may think of the combination of accident and preselection that yields particular people at particular places in particular organized systems—that interplay of levels, between the intrapersonal and the social/systemic, that our Gestalt model is particularly well organized to address. Some organizations, some families for example, are particularly gifted, for whatever reason, with just those complementary role representatives that support and "free up," as we have seen, the dominant contact mode of the system (which after all may well be "one-sided," in terms of our traditional "list of resistances"). On the other hand, such complementary (or, significantly, "outside") positions may be very stressful to the individuals concerned; and then part of the change agent's job may well be to educate the system as a whole to appreciate and support those necessary, atypical members, who may well be particularly subject to "burnout" (and here the notion of "identified patient" comes to mind). In this training group, for example, even a slight accidental change in membership might have yielded quite a different ground. As it was, the strongest members were all "good boys and girls"—which is to say, they could cheat, but they weren't very good at it! On the other hand, "strong member" itself is a notion which interacts with and has its full meaning only in a particular ground. As the ground of this group began to shift, leadership roles too began to change, and be shared out. Some members who had low prestige under the old "ground rules" (they were too "mousy," in the group's lingo) gained status with the change in the structure of expectations; others grew more uncomfortable, and less influential (that is, to say, the fairly un-common ability to form resistant interpersonal figures without im-mediate support was no longer the only coin of the realm, and those earlier leaders then had to experiment with other contact possibilities, with varying results).

No surprisingly, the initial conflict which the group had now role-structured so elaborately and so unspontaneously never really got off the ground, as it were—rather like those children's fantasy games where all the effort goes into the staging and group alloca-tion of roles, which turn out to be satisfying in someway in themselves. (Indeed, this kind of substitute exploration may serve many of the same needs, of location and articulation of support, as the conflict itself—and thus may the thought of usefully as a conflict reduction or resolution model in its own right, in other circumstances. The UN, for example, comes to mind, where much of what goes on is of this nature.) But other, subsequent conflicts did emerge, and were energized more fully and spontaneously— much to the alarm, in some cases, of a group that had formerly prided itself on being "good at conflict" and not much else. Now they began to understand, as we continued our analysis of figure and ground, that the *withholding of confluent contact* can itself function as an *avoidance of differentiation* and that an unloving system may be unloving because it is afraid to fight, just as the "unresistant" system may be afraid, in some sense, to love. Some of the old fighters in the group turned out to be good lovers as well; others not, or not so easily. Some of the new lovers (in the soft sense here) now emerged as good fighters too, under more loving ground conditions; others had to come to grips with struc-tural problems in their own personal ground, which were block-ing the emergence of resistant figure even under the new ground conditions. All of them reported that their understanding of and relation to the term "Gestalt" had been significantly destructured at least,—pending further personal reorganization.

C O N C L U S I O N

ND SO we come in a sense full circle. Experience, in the richly suggestive insight of the earliest Gestaltists, is always organic, never atomized. A choatic organization, in the words of Sonia March Nevis, leads to a chaotic experience. And this organization itself, chaotic or otherwise, can be analyzed, studied, destructured experientially and then put back together (or rather, allowed to restructure itself in the light of the new awareness, since that organizing process is the very nature of the "organism," in Goldstein's language, and cannot be prevented). All this is the very heart and meaning of our Gestalt perspective, on behavior and change, first fully articulated by Goodman, out of Perls's intuitive ground.

Even more broadly, *any* particular organization of experience will favor and support certain figures of contact, certain contact functions or styles, over others, which in turn will yield certain kinds of outcomes and not others, which may or may not fit with the desires and goals of the organism at hand, individual or systemic. Harmony among these terms is satisfaction, or health; disharmony, dissatisfaction, is, by definition, dysfunction. But, in the old psychodynamic landscape metaphor, this organization, this contact style, is contained "in" the ground (in process terms, we may say that these structures are the ground). Thus it is to those structures and that ground—and not to figure formation and figure destruction alone—that we must look, to understand the health or dysfunction of a particular person or system. The study of figures of contact, so richly elaborated and so productively applied by the Cleveland School in particular, is enhanced and rounded out by direct consideration of the underlying, *dynamically structured ground*. That is the whole argument of this book.

Why has this second, complementary pole of Gestalt analysis been relatively neglected in Gestalt writing down the years since Goodman's time? Chapters II and III considered some of the historical reasons, while Chapters I and V in particular were concerned with supplying some of the missing theoretical ground, drawing in part on the work of Lewin and Goldstein. But the reorganization of ground, theoretically speaking, that follows from this heightened awareness, opens the structural possibility of a new conceptual understanding, a new contact figure, of what had been called up to now the "resistances," but which we have preferred to think of in this perspective as *contact functions*, those necessary structural possibilities without which no contact at all (or only certain kinds of contact figure) can arise and achieve resolution. This model in turn then frees us up to begin, at least, to discuss the interplay of "personality" and systemic dynamics in the same terms—one of the long-sought grails of the social sciences, which Goodman hinted long ago should be among the achievements of the Gestalt perspective (indeed, his implication, at least, is that the very inability to do this freely is one of the signs of an "inadequate theory of awareness"). And then health and dysfunction, and intervention for change, whether on the individual or the systemic level, become a matter of the relation of those ground features, that structured contact repertory or style, to the values and goals of that person, that given system, in that particular field.

Today we live as the beneficiaries and heirs of a revolution which Goodman and Perls, among many others, shaped and led. From a time of resistance and destructuring of rigid institutions of the past, many of them constrictive or even life-threatening, we have moved to a time of searching for new organizations of purpose, new social dynamics, new habits and systems of feeling and thought (and again, it is always Goodman who reminds us that that categorization of the world itself, into "inner" and "outer" fields, is pernicious and illusory). Not that the old structures are gone. On the contrary, basic poles of experience, whole worlds of thought and emotion, are at war within us and around us, in restless search of new and more satisfying organization: individualism and community, altruism and greed, nationalism and world-awareness, spontaneity and steadfastness of purpose, hope and despair themselves (which are in the end but the twin Gestalt poles of figure formation and figure destruction, both necessary to life and both requiring to be brought into balance, which is to say expressed in the governance of ground).

But what then is to guide us in our search, if everything is in question? Are all figures equal, so long as they are fully energized, fully lived out; and is our Gestalt model equally hospitable to all of them? Or are there certain values, certain commitments, which are inherent to the ground of the Gestalt perspective, and thereby useful to us at that boundary or point of contact and integration between clear thinking and right action—both of which must in some sense be expressions and descriptions of our fullest selves? The old Perls/Goodman quest for a "value-free" psychotherapy would seem to incline toward the former position (see for example Perls et al., 1951, p. 329); certain of their themes and commitments, on the other hand—to passion, community, even life itself—seem clearly to cut the other way. Which of these contradictory positions is "Gestalt"? What is the nature of the connection, if any, between our descriptive theory of process and the urgent ethical figures in our lives? The answer, when it comes, must emerge from considerations of *structured ground*. In the words of Isadore From, "If your descriptive system is true, and your system of values is true, then there must be a connection between them" (From, 1988, personal communication).

It is up to us to find that connection, that balance and integration between a valid descriptive model of human process, and a humane way of life. The articulation of that boundary, that point of contact and structured union, between a living psychology and a living ethics, emerges as a pregnantly unfinished task from the ground of our revised Gestalt model.

References

Argyris, C., & Schon, D. (1978). *Organizational learning: a theory of action perspective*. Reading, Mass: Addison-Wesley.

Arnheim, R. (1949). The Gestalt theory of expression. In Henle, M. (Ed.), *Documents of Gestalt Psychology*. Berkeley: University of California Press (1961).

——— (1959). *Art and visual perception; a psychology of the creative eye*. Berkeley: University of California Press.

Barlow, A. R. (1981). Gestalt—antecedent influence or historical accident. *The Gestalt Journal*, IV(2), 35–54.

Beisser, A. R. (1970). The paradoxical theory of change. In Fagan, J. & Shepherd, I. (Eds.), *Gestalt therapy now*. Palo Alto, CA: Science and Behavior Books.

Bergler, E. (1956). *Homosexuality: disease or way of life?* New York: Collier Books.

Bion, W. R. (1958). *Experiences in groups and other papers*. New York: Basic Books.

Brown, G. & Merry, U. (1987). *The neurotic behavior of organizations*. New York: Gardner Press/Gestalt Institute of Cleveland Press.

Burke, W. (1980). Systems theory, gestalt therapy, and organizational development. In Cummings, T. (Ed.), *Systems theory for organizational development*. New York: John Wiley & Sons.

Crocker, S. (1981). Proflection. *The Gestalt Journal* IV(2), 13–34.

Crocker, S. (1983). Truth and foolishness in the 'gestalt prayer.' *The Gestalt Journal* VI(1), 4–16.

Davidove, D. M. (1985). The contribution of Paul Goodman. *The Gestalt Journal*, VIII(1), 72–77.

Ehrenfels, von C. (1890). Ueber Gestaltqualitaeten (On gestalt properties). *Vierteljahresschrift fuer Philosophie* 14.

Erikson, E. (1951). *Childhood and society*. New York: Norton.

Exner, A. (1894). *Entwurf zu einer physiologischen Erklaerung der psychischen Erscheinungen (Sketch for a physiological explanation of psychic appearances)*. Vienna: Deutike.

Fagan, J. (1970). The tasks of the therapist. In Fagan, J. & Shepherd, I. (Eds.), *Gestalt therapy now*. New York: Science and Behavior Books.

Fantz, R. E. (1975). Fragments of gestalt theory. Unpublished manuscript (available in reprint from the Gestalt Institute of Cleveland).

——— (1987). Gestalt approach. In Fosshage, J. & Loew, C. (Eds.), *Dream interpretation*. New York: PMA Publishing Corp.

Fingarette, H. (1988). *Heavy drinking*. Berkeley: University of California Press.

Freud, A. (1937). *The ego and the mechanisms of defense*. New York: International Universities Press, Inc.

Freud, S. (1894). The neuro-psychoses of defence. In Strachey, J. (Ed.), *The standard edition*, 3, 45–61. London: Hogarth Press (1953-).

——— (1900). *The interpretation of dreams*. In Strachey, J. (Ed.), *The standard edition*, 4–5. London: Hogarth Press (1953-).

——— (1905). *Three essays on the theory of sexuality*. In Strachey, J. (Ed.), *The standard edition* 7. London: Hogarth Press (1953-).

——— (1914). The case of the wolf-man/from the history of an infantile neurosis. In Strachey, J. (Ed.), *The Standard edition*, 17, 7–122. London: Hogarth Press (1953-).

——— (1920). Beyond the pleasure principle. In Strachey, J. (Ed.), *The standard edition*, 18, 3–64. London: Hogarth Press (1953-).

——— (1923). The ego and the id. In Strachey, J. (Ed.), *The standard edition*, 19, 3–66. London: Hogarth Press (1953-).

——— (1930). *Civilization and its discontents*. In Strachey, J. (Ed.), *The standard edition*, 21. London: Hogarth Press (1953-).

——— (1938). *An outline of psychoanalysis*. In Strachey, J. (Ed.), *The standard edition*, 23. London: Hogarth Press (1953-).

——— (1985). *The complete letters of Sigmund Freud to Wilhelm Fliess*. Masson, J. M. (Ed.) Cambridge: Harvard University Press.

From, I. (1978). An oral history of Gestalt therapy, part 2: a conversation with Isadore From (conducted by Rosenfeld, E). *The Gestalt Journal*, I(2), 8–27.

Gelb, A. & Goldstein, K. (1918). Analysis of a case of figural blindness. In Ellis, W. (Ed.), *A source book of gestalt psychology*. London: Routledge & Kegan Paul, Ltd., 1938.

Gelb, A. & Goldstein, K. (1920). Zur Psychologie des optischen Wahrnehmungs und Erkennungsvorgangs (On the psychology of optical interpretation and recognition processes). In *Psychologische Analysen hirnpathologischer Faelle (Psychological analysis of brain-damage cases)*. Leipzig: no publisher listed.

Ginger, S. (1987). *La gestalt/une therapie du contact*. Paris: Hommes et Groupes Editeurs.

Glasgow, R. (1971). Interview with Paul Goodman. *Psychology Today*, Nov., 1971.

Goldstein, K. (1925). Zur Theorie der Funktion des Nervensystems (Towards a theory of the functioning of the nervous system). *Archiven fuer Psychiatrische und Nerven Krankheiten*, 74.

———— (1939). *The organism*. Boston: American Book Company.

———— (1940). *Human nature in the light of psychopathology*. Cambridge: Harvard University Press.

Goodman, P. (1942). *The empire city*. New York: Bobbs-Merrill.

———— (1947). *Communitas*. New York: Random House.

———— (1959). *Making do*. New York: Random House.

———— (1960). *Growing up absurd*. New York: Random House.

———— (1962). *Utopian essays and practical proposals*. New York: Random House.

———— (1966). *Five years*. New York: Brussel & Brussel.

———— (1977). *Nature heals: psychological essays*. Stoehr, T., Ed. New York: Free Life Editions.

Guntrip, H. (1971). *Psychoanalytic theory, therapy and the self*. New York: Basic Books, Inc.

Gurman, A. & Kniskern, D. (Eds.) (1981). *Handbook of family therapy*. New York: Brunner/Mazel.

Henle, M. (1978). Gestalt psychology and Gestalt therapy. *Journal of the History of the Behavioral Sciences*, 14, 23–32.

Herman, S. & Korenich, M. (1977). *Authentic management: a Gestalt orientation to organizations and their development*. Reading, Mass: Addison-Wesley.

Hilgard, E. & Bower, G. (1966). *Conditioning and learning*. New York: Appleton.

Ilich, I. (1971). *Deschooling society*. New York: Harper & Row.

Jung, C. (1939). Conscious, unconscious, and individuation. In McGuire, W. (Ed.), *The collected works of C. G. Jung*, 9(1). London: Routledge & Kegan Paul, Ltd. (1959).

Katz, D. (1911). Die Erscheinungsweisen der Farben und ihre Beeinflussung durch die individuelle Erfahrung (The appearances of colors and their influence through individual experience). *Zeitschrift fuer Psychologie*, 7.

Katzeff, M. (1977). *Comment se realiser dans la vie quotienne et professionelle (Self-realization in daily and professional life)*. Brussels: Multiversite.

Kepner, E. & Brien, L. (1970). Gestalt therapy and behavioristic phenomenology. In Fagan, J. & Shepherd, I. (Eds.), *Gestalt therapy now*. New York: Science and Behavior Books.

Kepner, J. (1987). *Body pocess: a Gestalt approach to working with the body in psychotherapy*. New York: Gardner Press/Gestalt Institute of Cleveland Press.

Koffka, K. (1915). Toward a foundation for perceptual psychology. In Ellis, W. (Ed.), *A source book of gestalt psychology*. London: Routledge & Kegan Paul, Ltd. (1938).

——— (1935). *Principles of Gestalt psychology*. New York: Harcourt, Brace & World, Inc.

Koehler, W. (1915). Optische Untersuchungen am Schimpansen und am Haushuhn (Optical investigations on the chimpanzee and the domestic chicken). *Berliner Abhandlung*, 1915, 3.

——— (1920). *Die physischen Gestalten in Ruhe und im stationaeren Zustand (Physical Gestalts at rest and under stationary conditions)*. Berlin: Braunschweig.

——— (1922). Zur Theorie der stroboskopischen Bewegungen (Toward a theory of stroboscopic motion). *Psychologische Forschung*, 3.

——— (1925). *The mentality of apes*. New York: Harcourt, Brace & World.

——— (1927). Zum Problem der Regulation (On the problem of regulation). *Roux Archiven fuer Entwicklungsmechanik* 112.

——— (1938). *The place of value in a world of facts*. New York: Liveright.

——— (1940). *Dynamics in psychology*. New York: Liveright.

——— (1947). *Gestalt psychology*. New York: Liveright.

——— (1959). *Gestalt psychology*. New York: Mentor Books (The New American Library of World Literature, Inc.)

Kohut, H. (1977). *The restoration of self*. New York: International Universities Press.

Krueger, F. (1913). Consonance and dissonance. *Journal of Philosophical and Psychological Scientific Method*, 10.

——— (1915). *Ueber Entwicklungspsychologie (On developmental psychology)*. Berlin: no publisher listed.

Latner, J. (1982). The thresher of time: on love and freedom in Gestalt therapy. *The Gestalt Journal* V(1), 20–38.

Latner, J. (1983). This is the speed of light: field and systems theories in Gestalt therapy. *The Gestalt Journal,* VI(2), 71ff.

Lewin, K. (1917). Kriegslandschaft (War landscape). *Zeitschrift Angewandter Psychologie,* 12, 440–7.

—— (1926). Vorsatz, Wille und Bedurfnis (Intention, will, and need. *Psychologische Forschung,* 7, 330–85.

—— (1935). *A dynamic theory of personality.* Adams, D. & Zener, K., transl. New York: McGraw-Hill Book Company.

—— (1936). *Principles of topological psychology.* New York: McGraw-Hill Book Company.

—— (1951). *Field theory in social science.* New York: Harper & Brothers.

MacIntyre, A. (1981). *After virtue.* Notre Dame: Notre Dame Press.

Mandler, J. & Mandler, G. (1964). *Thinking: from association to Gestalt.* New York: John Wiley & Sons.

Marrow, A. (1969). *The practical theorist: the life and work of Kurt Lewin.* New York: Basic Books, Inc.

Martius, G. (1912). Ueber analytische und synthetische Psychologie (On analytic and synthetic psychology). *Berliner Kongress* 5.

Maslow, A. (1954). *Motivation and personality.* New York: Harper & Brothers.

Melnick, J. & Nevis, S. (1986). Power, choice and surprise. The Gestalt Journal, IX(2), 43—52.

Merry, U. & Brown, G. (1985). Neurotic Mechanisms applied to organizations. The Gestalt Journal, VIII(2), 49–85.

Merry, U. & Brown, G. (1987). *The Neurotic Behavior of Organizations.* New York: Gardner Press/Gestalt Institute of Cleveland Press.

Miller, M. (1981). The future of gestalt therapy: a symposium (Miller, M., moderator). *The Gestalt Journal,* IV(1), 3–16.

Minuchin, S. (1974). *Families and family therapy.* Cambridge, Mass: Harvard University Press.

Morrison, A. (1987). The eye turned inward: shame and the self. In Nathanson, D. (Ed.), *The many faces of shame.* New York: Guilford Press.

Mueller, G. (1923). *Komplextheorie und Gestalttheorie (Complex theory and Gestalt theory).* Gottingen: University of Gottingen.

—— (1925). Einfluss des Weissgehaltes des Infeldes und Umfeldes auf die dem Infelde entsprechenden Erregungen (Influence of whiteness content of figure and ground on the reactions to the figure). *Zeitschrift fuer Psychologie,* 97.

Nathanson, D. (1987). *The many faces of shame.* New York: Guilford Press.

Nevis, E. (1983). Evocative and provocative modes of influence in the implementation of change. *The Gestalt Journal* VI(2), 5–12.

——— (1987). *Organizational consulting/a Gestalt approach.* New York: Gardner Press/Gestalt Institute of Cleveland Press.

Nevis, S. (1979). Opening address, 25th anniversary conference, Gestalt Institute of Cleveland.

——— (1981). How Gestalt therapy views couples, families, and the process of their psychotherapy (with Zinker, J.) Working paper, Center for the Study of Intimate Systems. Gestalt Institute of Cleveland.

——— (1983). Conversing about Gestalt couples' and family therapy. (with Warner, E.) *The Gestalt Journal* VI(2), 40—50.

——— (1985a). Bringing the background into the foreground. The Gestalt Journal, VIII(1), 61–64.

——— (1985b). The Gestalt theory of couple and family interaction. (with Zinker, J.) Working paper, Center for the Study of Intimate Systems. Gestalt Institute of Cleveland.

——— (1986a). Intimacy and play in long-term relationships. (with Nevis, E. & Zinker, J.) Working paper, Center for the Study of Intimate Systems. Gestalt Institute of Cleveland.

——— (1986b). Finding the middle ground. Working paper, Center for the Study of Intimate Systems. Gestalt Institute of Cleveland.

Nevis, S. & Zinker, J. (1990). Couples and family therapy/a Gestalt approach. Unpublished manuscript.

Ovsiankina, M. (1976). The resumption of interrupted activities. In deRivera, J. (Ed.), *Field theory as human science.* New York: Gardner Press.

Perls, F. (1947). *Ego, hunger and aggression.* London: Allen & Unwin, Ltd.

——— (1969a). *Gestalt therapy verbatim.* Moab, Utah: Real People Press.

——— (1969b). In and out of the garbage pail. Moab, Utah: Real People Press.

——— (1971). Gestalt therapy. In Bry, A. (Ed.), *Inside psychotherapy.* New York: Basic Books, Inc.

——— (1973). *The gestalt approach and eye witness to therapy.* Palo Alto: Science and Behavior Books.

Perls, F., Hefferline, R. & Goodman, P. (1951). *Gestalt therapy/excitement and growth in the human personality.* New York: Julian Press.

Perls, L. (1982). An oral history of Gestalt therapy, part 1. *The Gestalt Journal* V(2), 9–31.

——— (19xx). *Leben an der Grenze.*

Petermann, B. (1932). *The Gestalt theory and the problem of configuration.* London: Routledge & Kegan Paul, Ltd.

Piaget, J. (1947). *Intelligence.* New York: Basic Books.

Polster, E. (1966). A contemporary psychotherapy. *Psychotherapy: Theory, Research & Practice,* III(1), 1–6.

——— (1985). Imprisoned in the present. *The Gestalt Journal,* VIII(1), 5–22.

——— (1986). A contemporary psychotherapy (rev). *The Gestalt Journal,* IX(2), 30–43.

Polster, E. & Polster, M. (1973). *Gestalt therapy integrated.* New York: Brunner/Mazel.

Rank, O. (1958). *Beyond psychology.* New York: Dover.

Reiff, C. (1962). *Freudian Psychology.* New York: Mentor Books.

Roazen, P. (1976). *Freud and his followers.* New York: Alfred A. Knopf.

Rosenblatt, D. (1980). This is Laura's book for her 75th birthday. *The Gestalt Journal,* III(1), 5–15.

——— (1988). What has love got to do with it? *The Gestalt Journal,* XI(1), 63–76.

Sacks, O. (1986). *The man who mistook his wife for a hat.* Yarmouth, Mass: J. Curley.

Shapiro, E. (1985). An oral history of Gestalt therapy: part 4. *The Gestalt Journal,* VIII(2), 5–26.

Schumann, F. (1900). Beitraege zur Analyse der Gesichtswarnehmung (Comments on the analysis of visual perception). *Zeitschrift fuer Psychologie* 23.

Schur, M. (1972). *Freud: living and dying.* New York: International Universities Press.

Sherrill, R. (1986). Gestalt therapy and Gestalt psychology. *The Gestalt Journal,* IX(2), 53–66.

Simkin, J. & Yontef, G. (1984). Gestalt therapy. In Corsini, R. (Ed.), *Current psychotherapies.* Ithaca, Ill: Peacock.

Smuts, J. (1926). *Holism and evolution.* New York: Macmillan.

Sullivan, H. (1953). *The interpersonal theory of psychiatry.* New York: W. W. Norton.

Wertheimer, M. (1912). Experimentelle Studien ueber das Sehen von Bewegungen (Experimental studies in the perception of motion). *Zeitschrift fuer Psychologie,* 61.

——— (1922). Untersuchungen zur Lehre von dem Gestalt (Investigations in the theory of Gestalt). *Psychologische Forschung* I.

——— (1925). Gestalt theory. In Ellis, W. (Ed.), *A source book of*

Gestalt psychology. London: Routledge & Kegan Paul, Ltd. (1938).

——— (1935). Some problems in the theory of ethics. In Henle, M. (Ed.), *Documents in Gestalt psychology.* Berkeley: University of California Press (1961).

——— (1959). *Productive thinking* (2nd ed). New York: Harper & Row (1st ed. 1945).

Wertheimer, M. M. (1964). Wertheimer, Max. In *Encyclopedia Britannica,* 23, 514–5.

Winnicott, D. (1988). *Holding and interpretation.* New York: Grove Press.

Wysong, J. (1985). An oral history of Gestalt therapy: part 4. *The Gestalt Journal,* VIII(2), 5–26.

Wysong, J. & Rosenfeld, E. (1982). *An oral history of Gestalt Therapy.* Highland, NY: The Gestalt Journal Press.

Yalom, I. (1977). The impact of a weekend group experience on individual therapy. *Archives of General Psychiatry,* 34(4), 399–415.

Yalom, I. (1970). *Theory and practice of group psychotherapy.* New York: Basic Books, Inc.

Zeigarnik, B. (1927). Ueber das Behalten von erledigten und unerledigten Handlungen (On the persistence of finished and unfinished tasks). *Psychologische Forschung,* 9, 1–85.

Zinker, J. (1977). *Creative process in Gestalt therapy.* New York: Brunner/Mazel.

Zinker, J. & Nevis, S. (see Nevis, S.)

Index of Names

ABOUT THE AUTHOR

Gordon Wheeler, Ph.D., combines many years of clinical experience with a long-standing interest in systems dynamics and organizational issues. Following training under psychodynamic, object relations, and social psychology models, he studied with followers of Perls and Goodman at the Gestalt Institute of Cleveland, and followers of Lewin at NTL. Drawing on Lewin's work, Wheeler uses the Gestalt model to integrate the intrapsychic, interpersonal, and systemic dynamics of intervention for change. A member of the faculty of the Gestalt Institute of Cleveland, he teaches the Gestalt model widely in both Europe and the United States. He is the author of several works of fiction, and translator of the forthcoming *Collective Silence* from Gardner Press, a work dealing with psychotherapeutic issues with children of Nazis. Wheeler lives in Cambridge, Mass., with his wife and five children.